A Walk With God

Living the Overcoming and Limitless Life

Dr. Dara M. Lemite

A Walk With God: Living the Overcoming and Limitless Life

Copyright © 2014 by Dr. Dara M. Lemite

ISBN 10: 0692287760
ISBN 13: 978-0-692-28776-7

Book Cover & Design by OnPath Graphics

Printed in the United States of America

Dedication

To my Mom and Dad, who have always loved and supported me, there are not enough ways to thank you! I thank God every day for such wonderful parents!

To my sister, Lisa, I am so thankful that you are in my life. God broke the mold when He created a sister like you! Love you always!

To my son, Matthew, you are the reason why I do what I do. I pray that you will know your God-given purpose and pursue it relentlessly!

Table of Contents

Acknowledgements

First and foremost, I want to give honor and glory to my Lord and Savior Jesus Christ. Without Him, I am nothing, and can do nothing. I thank Him for the inspiration to write this book.

To Minister Vivian Allen, I was blessed to have you in my life. You taught me that "The breaking of you, is the making of you". My life has been changed forever! I will never forget the wisdom you imparted to me. May you rest in peace.

To my family and close friends who have always supported me, you have always been a source of encouragement. I am thankful for your belief in me.

This book would not be possible, if it were not for the following people: I would like to thank Robert Ballat for giving me the push forward after taking your writer's workshop. I would like to thank Ebony Murrell of OnPath Graphics for such a wonderful book cover. Your work is awesome! I would like to thank my editor, Monique Nixon, who pays attention to every detail! I would also like to thank a fellow author, Shevita Cooper, who shared her insight and guidance as I was developing my book.

A special thank you, to Dr. Victor Seltzer, CFO of LS Management, who manages my various music endeavors. I am so thankful for you!

And, I would also like to thank D. Ellis, CEO of LS Management.

Introduction

Have you ever felt as if things were not going right? Have you ever felt incomplete inside? Have you ever thought, is this all there is to life? Do you want a change? Are you satisfied with what the world has to offer? Do you feel purposeful? Do you know that you have a divine destiny? Do you know that there is a purpose, a plan for your life? Well, if you have pondered these several questions presented to you, then you need to know and find your God-given purpose.

From the moment you were born, actually before you were even a thought in your parents' mind, you had a date with destiny. That destiny is God and His divine plan for your life. This book is to help you understand and find God's purpose for your life, not man's purpose. Please understand that God's purpose for your life and man's purpose are very different. God's purpose will lead you to a life of salvation and abundance, while man's purpose will lead you to a path of destruction. *"For I know the plans I have for you,"* declares the Lord, *"plans to prosper you and not harm you, plans to give you hope and a future."* (Jeremiah 29:11 NIV) *"I have come that they may have life, and life abundantly."* (John 10:10 NIV)

We are God's children; He loves us and will take care of us. If God is for us, who can be against us? Our light afflictions are for a moment. We are to look on the things that are unseen, for the Bible says the things which are seen are temporary, and the things which are unseen are eternal. Do you know what temporary means? Temporary means that it is subject to change, not permanent. Eternal means forever. As a child of God, you are qualified to live an overcoming and limitless life. In His word, He states that we are more than conquerors. Do you know what that means? It means that we have won the battle before it even began! A conqueror is one who overtakes, one who is powerful, one who is undefeated, and one who is unchallenged. This means that you can rise above and beyond your circumstances. This book will give you tools on how to live the overcoming and limitless life by walking with God.

Chapter 1

KNOWING GOD

In the beginning was the Word, and the Word was with God, and the Word was God.
(John1:1)

I truly believe in order to live an overcoming and limitless life we need to know God. Everything in life begins and ends with God. He is the Alpha and the Omega. He is the author and finisher of our faith. In order to know God, you must come in to relationship with Jesus Christ. The Bible says, *"No one comes to the Father but through Jesus."*(John 14:6) There are no shortcuts to God. We need to have Jesus as Lord and Savior over our lives. By knowing God, you will learn His will, His character, and His ways. All of this starts with studying, meditating, and learning the word of God. When you study the word of God, the Word will speak to you.

Knowing God is having a deep relationship and fellowship with Him. When you begin to know God, you are no longer an associate of Him, but you begin to know Him on a more intimate level. Think of the personal relationships you have: parents, spouse, siblings, friends, relatives, etc. In order to know these people well, you have to spend time in their presence. As you begin to know them, you learn their likes and dislikes, hopes and fears, and so on. There are certain qualities in personal relationships that are similar to a relationship with God.

When you know someone intimately, you can confide in them knowing that what you share with them, they will keep it to themselves. When we know God, we confide in Him our heart's deepest desires. We do this through prayer. Prayer is simply having a conversation with God. When we pray, we speak to God, but

He also speaks to us. *"For I am confident of this very thing, that He who began a good work in you will perfect it until the day of Christ Jesus."* Philippians 1:6 (NASB)

Another attribute in a relationship is trust. When you have trust in someone, you know that what they say they will do, they will do. When you trust God, you no longer doubt His promises working in your life. It may take time, but because you trust God, you know He is at work! *"Be strong and courageous, do not be afraid or tremble at them, for the Lord your God is the one who goes with you. He will not fail you or forsake you."* Deuteronomy 31:6 (NASB)

Love is key to any successful relationship. Just like a parent loves a child, God loves you immensely. You must know this. As a mother, I would give anything to make sure my son is well. I love him more than words can say. God loves us this way also, but so much greater than we can ever imagine. *"For*

God so loved the world, that he gave his only Son, that whoever believes in him should not perish but have eternal life." John 3:16 (NIV)

Along with love, comes friendship. Friendships are stronger than an association with someone. In friendship, there is a love and a commitment to enhancing the relationship. Throughout life, we have friendships. Our friendships are dear to us, and we hold them close to our heart. God loves us with an everlasting love, and He calls us His friends. *"And the scripture was fulfilled that says, "Abraham believed God, and it was credited to him as righteousness," and he was called God's friend* James 2:23 (NIV)

Dependability is important to any successful relationship. If you are not able to depend on someone, how can you trust them? God is dependable. You can rely on God. He will never fail you. He will do exactly what He says He will do. He won't say one thing and then do another. God is not fickle, and He does not waver in His love for you. *"For I am the Lord, I change not."* Malachi 3:6

Accountability is the act of being responsible. When you are accountable to someone, you will hold up your end of the bargain. Meaning, you will not renege on what you say you will do. We are accountable to God. God is accountable to His word. We can rely and trust that His word will not change and will not fail. I am so thankful that God is not like man. From day to day, we change our opinions, feelings, emotions, etc., but God does not. *"God is not a man, that he should lie; neither the son of man, that he should repent: hath he said, and shall he not do it? Or hath he spoken, and shall he not make it good?"* Numbers 23:19

Expectation is the belief that something will happen. In relationships, we expect to be treated well, to be cared for, and to be loved. As believers, God expects that we will read His word, and follow His commandments. One of the greatest commandments is to love one another. God expects us to love one another. We should treat others with love and kindness. In the same way, we can expect that God will treat us with love and kindness. Why? Because it is in His word, and His word never fails. *"So shall My word be that goes forth from My mouth; It shall not return to Me void, But it shall accomplish what I please, And it shall prosper in the thing for which I sent it."* Isaiah 55:11 (NKJV)

Manipulation is not a positive attribute in a relationship. Manipulation is influencing someone in an unfair manner. It is getting someone to do something they really do not want to do, but in doing so it will benefit you. Basically, it is trying to get your own way. God does not operate this way. You probably are wondering why I included this as an attribute. Some people feel that God causes negative things to happen in their life, to manipulate them to turn to Him. This friend, is not the case. God is love. He loved you before you were even a thought in your mother's mind. God does not manipulate us to do right. Now, is God a strong persuader? I believe so. But, God does not manipulate us to live a life according to His word. Manipulation is never beneficial in relationships, and it is definitely not beneficial in a relationship with God. *"Love is patient and kind; love does not envy or boast; it is not arrogant or rude. It does not insist on its own way; it is not irritable or resentful."* 1 Corinthians 13:4-5 (ESV)

Another attribute in a relationship is protection. When you love someone, you would never put them in harm's way. As a parent, I do everything in my power to keep my son safe. God loves us this way also, but so much more. God's love for us offers us divine protection. *"For he shall give his angels charge over thee, to keep thee in all thy ways."* ~Psalm 91:11

I would like to share a story with you. Growing up, I had a tremendous fear of dogs.

One day, my friend and I walked to the bus stop. I remember my Dad watched us as we walked to the bus stop. Out of nowhere, this big dog came across the street and was approaching us. I began to shake in fear. My friend said to me, "don't run." And of course, I bolted! As I began to run, the dog came after me. It seemed like time had stopped. The next thing I remember was hearing my Dad's voice. I remember my Dad, charging after the dog, and he kicked the dog. The dog ran back to its house. My fear went away instantly. My Dad asked if I was okay, and of course, I was a little shaken. As long as I live, I will never forget that day. My Dad showed me that he would protect me at all costs. This is a prime example of God's love for us. God will do and can do all that He can to make sure we are safe.

There are several key points you need to understand to know God personally:

Key 1: God loves you

God loves you and has a wonderful plan for your life. God gave up His only son, and allowed Him to die on the cross an agonizing death, so that you might have life. Once you accept Jesus Christ as your personal Lord and Savior, life takes on a new meaning. *"I came that they may have life, and have it abundantly."* ~ John 10:10 (NASB)

Key 2: Our sin separates us from God

No matter how good you may think you are, we all have fallen short of God's glory. Our sin has caused us to be separated from God. "If *anyone, then, knows the good they ought to do and doesn't do it, it is sin for them."* James 4:17 (NIV) We are all guilty of sin, and will be judged for our sin. The punishment for sin is eternal separation from God, which the Bible names, hell. Trying to be good, is not going to allow us to escape from hell. There is only one way, and that is Jesus. Once you become a believer, you receive the gift of eternal life.

Key 3: We all need Jesus

No matter how perfect and great you think your life is, we all need Jesus. He is the only provision for our sins. While we were still in sin, Jesus went to the cross and died for us. He died so that we may have everlasting life, with God our Father. The only way to God is through Jesus. *"I am the way, the truth, and the life. No one comes to the Father except through Me."* ~ John 14:6 (NKJV)

Key 4: Receive Jesus Christ as Lord and Savior

Once you receive Jesus Christ as Lord and Savior, you are able to experience the full benefits of being a believer. All of the wonderful promises in the Bible are yours, once you become a believer. *"For all the promises of God in Him are yes, and in Him Amen, to the glory of God through us."* 2 Corinthians 1:20 (NKJV). We receive Christ as Savior through faith. *"For it is by grace you have been saved, through faith—and this is not from yourselves, it is the gift of God."* Ephesians 2:8 (NIV)

The Mind of Christ

When you have the mind of Christ, you share in the plan, purpose, and perspective of Christ. This is something that all believers possess. *"For who hath known the mind of the Lord, that he may instruct him? But we have the mind of Christ."~* 1 Corinthians 2:16. Possessing the mind of Christ means that we do not think the way we did before. Our minds are transformed. When you have the mind of Christ you see things the way God sees them, rather than how you think they are. In order to have the mind of Christ, one must be saved. After salvation, a believer lives a life under God's influence. The mind of Christ is in sharp contrast to the wisdom of man. The mind of Christ involves wisdom from God, once hidden but now revealed. The mind of Christ is given to believers through the Spirit of God. The mind of Christ cannot be understood by non-believers. The mind of Christ gives believers discernment in spiritual matters. When you begin to think with the mind of Christ, you will begin to take on a new attitude. You will display certain qualities such as unselfishness, humbleness, obedience, and patience. Along with all of these attributes, you must possess a servant's heart.

My friends, there are only two ways to live this thing called life. Either you live it by your own way or by God's way. A self-led life means that you are on the throne, directing all of your decisions and actions. A self-led life has no room for God. People who lead self-led lives tend to believe that things just happen to them. They do not believe that their steps are ordered and that there is a greater power at work. Often, self-led people deny the existence of God. Also, self- led people feel that if there is a God, why He would allow such bad things to happen? This goes back to the garden and the fall of man. Because we live in a sin-filled world, bad things happen. Also, God has given us the gift of free will. He wants us to freely choose Him. God will not force us to worship and believe in Him.

On the other hand, a Christ- led life is one in which God is at the center. A person who lives a Christ-led life, allows God to guide them in their life. They pray and consult with God in the everyday routines of life. God is at the center. A person who leads a Christ- led life knows that they would not and could not exist without God. Their very being and essence depends on Him. People who live Christ-led lives know that their steps are ordered, and there are no coincidences or accidents. They believe that everything that has happened to them is a part of God's plan for their lives. "*And we know that all things work together for good to them that love God, to them who are the called according to his purpose."* Romans 8:28

Keys to Remember

- God Loves You
- Our Sin Separates Us From God
- We All Need Jesus
- Receive Jesus As Lord and Savior
- Only Two Ways to Live - Christ- Led or Self- Led

Chapter 2

STEP OUT ON FAITH

"Now faith is the substance of things hoped for, the evidence of things not seen."
Hebrews 11:1

In the movie, *Field of Dreams,* a voice whispers, "If you build it, they will come." Before there was any manifestation of the baseball field, Kevin Costner's character had to put his faith to work. Faith is putting what you believe into action, on purpose, expecting results! In order for faith to work, you have to exercise it on purpose and use it intentionally. There has to be a desire within you that is so great, that you will not allow what you see with your natural eyes to deter what your spirit believes. You have to keep pressing forward in spite of the obstacles, because you will reap if you faint not

24

(Galatians 6:9). Each person is dealt a measure of faith (Romans 12:3). Do not deny the voice of God within you.

I believe that sometimes people do not realize that they exercise faith in their daily routines. When you get ready to leave for work in the morning, you have faith that you will get in your car and it will start, or you have faith in mass transit to get you where you need to go. You have faith that when you sit down at your desk, that your chair will not drop from under you. You have faith in your boss that he will allow you to have a lunch break and hopefully leave on time. We use faith in the little things, so if we can trust God in that, how come we cannot trust Him for the big things in life? Everyone is exercising faith whether they know it or not. Some people exercise faith in believing for positive things to happen. Other people exercise faith in reverse, which is fear in believing negative things to happen.

Everyone has God given dreams. What good is it though, if we believe our dreams are great, but never take any action towards realizing those dreams? Faith requires action and persistence. You have to believe without a shadow of doubt that God will bring it to pass. The Bible says, "No good thing will he withhold from them that walk uprightly." Psalm 84:11

One of my friends is a successful entrepreneur. I asked him one day, "What is the key to your success?" He told me he lives by the *Leap Frog Theory* and explained how he just jumps out there and gives it a try. He said you will never know what you are capable of accomplishing if you never push yourself. He also told me before his business became successful, he envisioned it as such. My friend, the successful entrepreneur, said his desire was to work from home, be in business for himself, and live financially free. He said everyday he woke up, he kept his thoughts on success and abundance. He even took action

26

towards making his dreams a reality. Every day, he would sit at his computer and envision himself responding to clients and so on and so forth. Soon after, people started to call him for his services. It was not long after, that his business began to take off. He also told me that he had enough faith in his abilities to bring it to pass, and believed that God would help him.

A business associate of mine deals with high end investments. When I say high end, I mean deals that are worth millions of dollars! He always shares wonderful nuggets of wisdom with me. He is very enlightening. He shared with me one day, how he thought it was amazing how people will go through years and years of schooling to essentially work for someone else, but yet when you tell people about entrepreneurship, they believe it takes too long to become successful. He said it baffled him how a person can go hard, working for someone else for 40 years, but not take 3- 5 years going hard for themselves to be successful in their own business. I asked him what his secret, how he was so sure that he would "make it?" His reply, "I have faith in God and my abilities. Quitting is not an option." He continued, "If I were to give up, I might as well die. I truly believed I would make it, and I have." Faith requires stepping out of the norm. I always say to have something you've never had, you have to do something you've never done!

I truly believe nothing happens until there is a corresponding action towards what you want. Faith believes in what you want to come to pass, even when things look contrary to what you believe.

Often, our faith will be tested to see if we really want the thing we believe in. Faith requires patience in God's timing, not ours. We live in a microwave type society; where everything is prepared now and fast. We have to gain the patience to endure. Let me share another story with you.

One day, I needed something to eat and I decided to go through a drive thru at a popular fast food chain. There was a line of people waiting to place their order at the drive thru. As I sat in the drive-thru, it seemed like an infinite amount of minutes passed. At one point, I began to get frustrated. I decided I was going to leave. At that moment, the line started to move, and within a short matter of time, I placed my order. Deep within, I felt God say, "Don't give up when you are on the edge of a breakthrough." Often we give up just when things are about to turnaround in our situation. There is a saying that it is always darkest before dawn. People who have went through the greatest obstacles, achieve the greatest results! Hang in there! Have faith! Trust God! He is working on your behalf!

How to Grow Your Faith

In order to grow your faith, you need to have a relationship with God. This allows us to know God intimately. When we know God intimately, He will give us a revelation of His nature, His power, and our rights as His children. Also, it is important to know the word of God, which is the Bible. His Word is written in the Bible. Faith comes by hearing the word of God (Romans 10:17). Hearing the word of God will cause the Word to become deep rooted in your spirit. Another way to grow your faith is through praise. Praise is having a deep level of gratitude to God. Praise Him for what He is doing in your life, has done, and will do. The Bible also says that God inhabits the praises of His people (Psalm 22:3). Growing your faith, will require obedience. Obedience is submission to God's will. The Bible says that obedience is better than sacrifice (1 Samuel 15:22). Obedience means acting immediately on what God has told you to do. We grow our faith through our testimony. Our testimony will encourage other believers and non-believers as well. The Bible says "We overcome by the blood of the Lamb, and by the word of our testimony." (Revelation 12:11).

Vision

In Proverbs 29:18, it says, "Where there is no vision, the people perish." In biblical terms, vision means divine perspective or divine wisdom. An individual's sight depends on the lens he is looking through, and his hearing depends on the filter he listens from. This is why the Bible says, that "Faith comes by hearing, and by hearing the word of God." (Romans 10:17) When God puts a vision on your heart, you need to pursue it. Often, a vision is something that God places on your heart that will seem impossible to attain, but it will take your faith for it to come to pass. With God all things are possible! For example, when God put it on my heart to write this book, I thought it was impossible. I was like, there is no way I can do this! How can I accomplish something as big as writing a book! Little by little, I just started to write daily. I knew that I needed to get this book out, and that it would be cathartic for me. At first, I did not know all the details about what I was going to write. I put my faith in God and trusted that He would give me the insight and wisdom about what to write. I've learned that when you put your faith in God, He will give you clear directions on which way to go. God never fails; you need to put your faith in Him!

I remember when God gave me the vision to form an entertainment agency. Months before this happened, I had been praying for a business idea. One day, as I was driving, I felt the idea drop in my spirit to form an entertainment agency. In my mind, I thought of having my group, *Dara Marie Productions*, perform for different social events. I was thinking about weddings, retirement parties, corporate parties, and so on. I was not thinking about the entertainment industry. I first reacted feeling a little confused. I've never had a business before, never had an entertainment agency, where am I going to find the people to work with? How do I start? My mind raced and rattled with these questions. I realized that I needed to start somewhere, so I made business cards. Then, I began to pass out my cards. Every step from there was a step of faith. I didn't know exactly how everything was going to work, but I walked by faith. And, this is what God wants us to do. *"For we walk by faith, not by sight."* (2 Corinthians 5:7). Through faith, God began to open some incredible doors. I began to meet various recording artists and people in the entertainment industry. It was mind blowing! When you exercise your faith, God will move on your behalf. As people of

God, we need to take chances while exercising wisdom. By no means am I advocating for people to do things without thinking them through. However, on the other hand, if there is a dream burning within you, pursue it! You will never know what you are truly made of unless you jump out there and try!

It is important to have a vision for your life, because if you do not have a vision other things will dictate that for you. I believe having a life of vision is important because this will help with your stability. Even when the pressures of life hit, you will not be swayed because your vision is your anchor and it allows you to stay grounded. You will know where you are headed and what you want out of life.

Take a moment and think: What is your vision? Do you have goals, dreams, desires that you want to see come to pass? Brainstorm, imagine, and dream. Focus on the things that give your life purpose and meaning. Do not put limits on your vision. The Bible says, if we delight ourselves in Him, He will give us the desires of our hearts (Psalm 37:4). Start to think big and believe big! As you believe, see those things you are believing for as if they are already here. God is powerful and there is nothing that He cannot do.

As you are creating your vision, there is something you must understand. Everyone is not going to support your vision. There will be people that may feel intimidated and even try to stop you from moving forward. Your vision is something that should not be shared with everyone. *Know your circle.* Know who is for you and who is against you. Everybody does not want to see you succeed. That is okay. You will still proceed forward anyway. Do not allow people or things to get you sidetracked. Stay true to your vision!

The Bible instructs us to write the vision and make it plain. Write down a list of things you want to accomplish. I suggest you pinpoint 10 specific areas in which you want to improve.

You cannot measure what you have not written down or identified. Do your research in regards to your vision. For example, if you want to be a restaurateur, you will need to know what it will take to open and run a successful restaurant. Also, set goals. Put yourself on a time frame of when you want to accomplish your goals. Set deadlines and adhere to them. Procrastination is the enemy of success. We will talk about that in a later chapter. Also, understand as you are working towards your vision, it is a process. There will be a time where you will be waiting for your vision to come to pass.

I also encourage you to create a vision board. A vision board is a collection of pictures which show the goals you want to achieve. Create your vision board with things you are passionate about. The items included should be things you want to have, be, or do in life. Once your vision board is completed, place it where you can see it daily. Each day take several moments to look at your vision board. If you can, look at it several times a day. Your vision board will serve as a reminder of the goals you are working towards. By looking at it daily, it will help to keep your goals embedded in your mind. Another idea is a vision journal. I personally use a vision journal, because I don't want everyone seeing my vision. I believe words have power, and sometimes people can try to speak death to your vision, this is why I keep my vision in a journal. I also like a vision journal because it is private and portable. A vision journal is similar to a vision board in that you can cut out pictures of things you desire, or write out phrases based on what you want to accomplish in life. As you look at it, reflect on your goals and the images you have placed in your journal. Remember, what you think on consistently and persistently will show up in your life, it is only a matter of time. The mind is powerful. *"For as he thinketh in his heart, so is he."* (Proverbs 23:7)

Focus

I believe in order for your vision to come to pass it requires focus. Focus on the life you truly desire and deserve. Begin to meditate on God's word and speak His promises over your life and current situation. What are your dreams and goals for the future? What do you want your future to look like? What are things you hope to achieve during your lifetime? What are some things that you can do to make a positive change? When you focus on what you want, you will prosper. Write your goals down, plan your future. Be consistent and persistent in the things you want to accomplish. When you are focused on a goal, you will be resolute on accomplishing that specific goal.

I remember once having a conversation with my friend, Leonie Morency. She said to me, "Focus is paying attention to the assignment that is in front of you. God has a purpose and a plan for everybody. It is our job to find that purpose and focus on it."

I also remember once being asked to proctor an exam. Proctors were required to actively supervise the test by walking up and down the aisles of the classroom. At one point, my eyes began to glaze over. The room was quiet, children were working on the exam, and I began to feel tired. I heard the Lord say, "Stay focused. You're on an assignment." At that point, I felt more energized; I recalled there was a reason for me to be at that place at that time. Focus allows you to stay on task, and to not lose sight of what you need to focus on.

While you are focusing on your goal, it is important to remove distractions. Distractions will come in the form of people or situations. Anything that is moving you away from your goal is a distraction. You have to realize what is important to you and know what is worth your time. Remember, you are on a mission to fulfill the call of God on your life. You do not have time to get sidetracked. When you are focused, no matter what obstacles come your way, you will not be swayed to the left or right. *You will be like a tree planted by rivers of water, which brings forth its fruit in due season.* (Psalm 1:3)

Keys to Remember

- Identify your vision
- Dream Big
- Be Courageous
- Set Goals to Acquire Your Vision
- Do Your Research
- Understand the Process of Waiting
- Your Vision Propels You
- Give God the Glory for the Vision
- Expect the Manifestation

Chapter 3

FREEDOM FROM FEAR

"For God hath not given us the spirit of fear; but of power, and of love, and of a sound mind." 2 Timothy 1:7

It has been said that fear is False Evidence Appearing Real. Fear can be crippling, paralyzing, and cause you to stop right in your tracks. Having fear will block you from moving into the things God has called for you. There are several things you need to know about fear.

Fear Is Not Of God

We know that God is love, and He has not given us a spirit of fear. In His word, God gave us power, love, and a sound mind. Anything that does not line up with those attributes, do not let it dwell within you. In His word, it says that we are more than conquerors. A conqueror is not fearful. The Word also says

41

we can do all things through Christ. This means we have strength and power. Both of those attributes are not of fear. You are equipped and able to face any and every circumstance that comes your way. God is with you always. The phrase, "do not be afraid" is in the Bible 365 times! That is a daily reminder which could help you face fear each day of the year. God want us to live bold and empowered lives. When fear is present in our lives, it is a sure sign that we have not let go and let God do His work.

How do you say you are in Christ, yet speak fear, doom, hopelessness, and, insecurity? This is something that baffles me. There are people that say they are believers, yet they walk in fear. They speak fear over faith! This is something I do not understand. Be aware of things you say and also the thoughts you possess. You do not need to entertain every thought that drops in your mind, especially if it is a fear-filled thought! Stay alert because the devil wants you to live in fear. If you stay in fear, you cannot operate in faith. Be aware, my dear friends.

Fear Cancels Out Faith

How can you exercise your faith, if you are walking in fear? As I said earlier, fear is crippling and will cause you not to progress. If you are in a constant state of fear, you will not be able to truly live your God-given purpose. God has a specific plan for your life. You are called to do something greater than your current circumstance. You must know this and have this belief deep rooted in your heart and soul. Do you remember the story about Joshua and Caleb? Of the 12 spies, it was Joshua and Caleb that came back and said they could possess the land. The other people were too fearful to take that step. They told about the giants they saw, and that they were grasshoppers in their sight. I truly believe that what you believe, will affect the outcome of how you react to a situation. I always wonder had

43

the other spies felt the same way as Joshua and Caleb, they may have seen the promise fulfilled as well. I know at times it can be difficult, but at all costs, do not give in to fear!

Fear Paralyzes You

Allow me to share another story with you. Upon graduating high school, I was accepted into Hofstra University. I went there to study music education. When I began studying music at Hofstra, it was an eye-opening experience. During my high school years, I was one of the top flautists in the department. When I entered Hofstra, I was so shocked to find out there were many other great flautists! For some reason, anxiety started to set in. I do not know if it was because I was in a new school and environment. I remember getting ready for class and having knots in my stomach, Meanwhile, I was doing great in all of my classes and performing groups, however, little by little, the anxiety which was fear became overwhelming! I recall one day, my mother dropping me off to a band rehearsal, and I would not get out of the car! I sat there and cried. I told my mom how scared I felt, and that I could not go to the rehearsal. I was paralyzed by fear! That day, I missed the rehearsal and went home. I could not understand how something I loved so much was causing such mind crippling fear. The fear became worse. I remember that first semester, staying in the library for hours to study, but also because of my anxiety, I wanted to be alone. The fear I had was so great that I did not want to be in social settings. I remember starting to feel very conscious about myself and began to have low self- esteem. I started to have so many irrational thoughts. I started to doubt myself, my musical abilities, and just felt that I was not good enough. This was not the truth. I started to tell myself that I was not good enough to be in the music department, not a good flautist, and that I should drop out of school! I was causing myself unnecessary pressure. Meanwhile, I was having good grades, and I was still an awesome flautist! This fear I had clouded reality! In reality, I was a great flautist, a great student, and had great capabilities. But fear is a lie from the pit of hell, and it will cause you to not see things clearly! Because of this, my parents became very concerned. I thank God for my parents because throughout this whole process, they never left my side and was very supportive. They felt I needed to talk with someone. They contacted my pastor at the time. I sat and talked with him. He prayed with me and gave me godly advice. After talking with him several times, I overcame my anxiety. I now realize it was an irrational fear, and I needed to get through the process. I thank God I am free from fear. God makes all things new!

Fear stops Progression

Fear clouds your judgment. When you are fearful, you will not be able to make sound decisions. Fear will keep you stuck. It will keep you from God's best. Fear will have you at a stand-still instead of moving forward. Fear will keep you looking back as if your best days were behind you instead of in front of you. It can cause you to give up on your goals, dreams, and vision. Fear halts progress. Often, the fear that we may have is because of the thoughts we think and our self-talk. What have you been thinking on lately? What are you saying about your life? Are you speaking words that edify, or words of self-doubt and defeat?

Do not give into your fear, give into your faith. Sometimes, we have fear of what others think about us. I know I used to worry about how other people felt about me. I was so concerned about other people's view of me, that I didn't ask, what do I think about me? Do not worry about what other people think. It is important to not live your life based on other people's opinions. If you do, you will remain paralyzed. You cannot control who is going to like you and who does not. At the end of the day, if you are doing what God has called you to do, it does not matter what people have to say.

The reality of the situation is this: caskets do not have bunk beds. When your earthly life is over, no one is going with you. You are going out alone. This is something you have to understand. Mediocrity is offended by greatness. People will try to stop you from going to the next level. Sometimes, it is because they lack the courage that you have and silently wish they had the courage to make such moves. Or, sometimes they may have a fear of trying to move forward. Either way, fear halts progress. It will stop the call and plan of God for your life. As I said earlier, God did not give us the spirit of fear. Fear is a lie from the pit of hell! If the devil can get you to believe his lies then you will stop moving forward and not fulfill God's purpose for your life.

People are not the author and finisher of our faith, God is. You have to believe that God has a great plan for you and that you are destined for greatness and success. Please do not let fear stop your progress in life. Decide to have a clear vision for your life. By doing so, you will not allow people or circumstances to dictate that vision for you. I have learned that sometimes you have to stop talking to people and start talking to God. By no means am I saying to not seek wise counsel, but at the same time use discernment. Make sure the people that are speaking into your life are of the same mindset, hold the same values, and have an indelible vision for themselves. *"Indeed, the very hairs of your head are all numbered. Don't be afraid; you are worth more than many sparrows"* (Luke 12:7 NIV).

Keys to Remember

- Fear is not of God
- Fear Cancels out Faith
- Fear Paralyzes You
- Fear Stops Progression
- Fear hinders positive thinking

Chapter 4

LIVE ON PURPOSE

"And we know that all things work together for good to them that love God, to them who are the called according to his purpose." ~ Romans 8:28

While alive, live! Each day is a gift and it is filled with meaning and purpose. As long as you are breathing and have a pulse God has a plan and purpose for you. It is our job to find that purpose and fulfill it. I do not believe God put us here to wander aimlessly through life and just go through the motions. I truly believe that we are called to something greater than ourselves. We are co-heirs and co-creators with God. You are an original design; there are no duplicate copies. Your children may have your genes, but they are unique, too!

When you live your life on purpose, each day is designed with a goal in mind. Each day you arise with anticipation and expectation. Due to your relationship with God, you know there is an assignment for you to do. There are certain things you may be striving towards. When you live on purpose, you find out what the true meaning of life is and then you live it. Things are not done haphazardly when you live life on purpose. You do things with an end goal in mind. For example, people who purposely go on a diet, they do so with the intention to lose weight. People who start a business do it with the intention to make money. When you live life on purpose, you do things intentionally. Iyanla Vanzant once said, "Your purpose gave birth to you. It has molded and shaped who you are and what you do. Your purpose is the reason you live and breathe. Your purpose guides your heart, hands, and head. It is alive in you. It is there within, that you must seek to know it and live it."

I remember when I first joined various social media platforms, I joined them with the sole purpose of advertising myself. I purposely placed my pictures on these sites advertising myself as a flutist. I did this on purpose. My goal was to receive inquiries from people who needed a live musician at their event. I did not join these sites for a hobby; I did it with a purpose. I put myself out there on purpose, with the intention of getting a response. I attended events with the intention to network on purpose. I call it "partying with a purpose". I'm not there just to sit and make small talk and laugh for a few hours, I have a goal in mind. I deliberately seek out new business connections. I purposely meet goal-oriented people. My motto is, "If I cannot learn from you, what purpose can you serve?" I believe people should add value to your life, and you should do the same in turn. When you realize there is a mandate and a mission for your life, there is no time for games! Align yourself with people who are doing better than you. Learn from people who know more than you, and people who have achieved what you are trying to achieve. From what I have observed, successful people seek out like-minded people on purpose. They understand the power of intention and purpose. Please understand when you change the way you do things, the things you do will change.

A friend of mine decided that she needed a lifestyle change. Her health was being affected negatively. She decided to begin a diet and exercise plan. She changed her eating habits, and decided to incorporate exercise into her daily routine. Every day, she would wake up early and ride her bike for several miles. She decided to give up soda, dessert, and other sugar filled foods. As time passed, she started to feel significantly better, lost weight, and saw tremendous results. She told me if she had not made that decision on purpose, she probably would have never changed. She said if she had not made those changes, Diabetes, and other health issues were imminent. She is a wife and mother, and she knows she has to be in good health not only for herself but also for her family. She intentionally made a life changing decision that turned her life around for the better.

One of my business associates, shared a few key things with me one day. He said when doing business, there are some things you must do on purpose. First, you have to know your circle. The people you choose to partner with must match your ambition, drive, work ethic, and accountability. He also said to select people who are problem solvers and visionaries. I asked him to elaborate a little more. He said problem solvers figure out solutions to problems. Often times, it does not take them a long time to come up with a solution to a problem. They are vital to a business. Also, he said visionaries think large! It actually offends them to think small. They will help to create a grand vision for your business on purpose due to the very nature of who they are. He explained to me that these two types of people go hand in hand. My friend told me to select people who display those qualities. He told me to seek those kinds of people purposely. When you do things purposefully, there is no time for hesitation, distraction, or procrastination, He reiterated. Like the popular Nike slogan states, Just Do It! You need to get moving and stay focused. He explained that people who become successful, become successful on purpose. Also, you need to be transparent on purpose with clients as well as partners, or associates. People value truth.

I intend to be successful on purpose. When I began to get serious about my goals, I decided a few things had to change. I started to have more alone time intentionally. It was not that I did not want to be around people, but I knew in order to get done what I needed to do, I needed to be alone to focus. I also understood that time is of the essence. I had to get moving quickly to make these goals happen. I decided on purpose that I was not going to spend time idling.   Please understand, time does not wait for anyone. There is no dress rehearsal for life. Do what you can, while you can.   While you can, you must evolve and grow, or else you will remain stagnant. Slow down and appreciate each day of your life. Look at each day as a gift. When you do that, the ordinary becomes the extraordinary.   Make up your mind to set goals on purpose, then proceed to demolish them!   I wrote this book on purpose, with the intention that it would open a person's mind to the greatness held within.

When you truly seek to live your life on purpose, that is when doors begin to open. As I said earlier, we are co-creators with God. Everything you need to be successful is within you!   Living on purpose requires action. You cannot sit idle and watch life pass you by. You need to go after the things God has placed on your heart. I have heard people say: "Eventually it will all fall into place." On the contrary, I believe we have to make things fall into place. As people of God, we have to make our goals happen and take action. Also, if it is not part of your purpose, do not make it part of your plan. This means do not waste time on things that will keep you stagnant. When you live life on purpose, you are always moving, changing, and growing into what God has called you to be. When you live life on purpose, you are no longer dwelling on the past; you are looking toward the future. Here is a poem I wrote titled, "On Purpose".

On Purpose

Live on purpose,

Pray on purpose,

Love on purpose,

Forgive on purpose,

Be Kind on purpose,

Give on purpose,

Be wise on purpose,

Be determined on purpose,

Be focused on purpose,

Be courageous on purpose,

Be tenacious on purpose,

Be vigilant on purpose.

Keys to Remember

- Life is a gift
- God has a plan for you
- God has embedded gifts in you
- Set goals on purpose
- Live on intention
- Time waits for no one
- Know your circle
- Align yourself with goal-oriented people
- Success is within you

Chapter 5

WALK IN YOUR DIVINE NATURE

"Truly I tell you, whatever you bind on earth will be bound in heaven, and whatever you loose on earth will be loosed in heaven."~ Matthew 18:18 (NIV)

As humans, God created us triune in nature. We have a spirit, soul, and body. We know we are triune in nature, because God said, "Let us make man in our image." (Genesis 1:26). As a believer, God has given us authority over all the works of the enemy according to Luke 10:19. The word authority literally means power. God has given us power that we can affect change in the natural and spiritual realm. This authority allows us to govern our lives and circumstances. God has also given us dominion. (Genesis 1:26) Dominion means to have charge over. Jesus died on the cross so that we may live an overcoming and abundant life. No matter what challenges you may face, you have the authority to change things around you.

Who You Are In Christ

When you received Jesus Christ as Lord and Savior, the old has passed away and all things have become new (2 Corinthians 5:17). Also, you have been delivered from the power of darkness (Colossians 1:13). As a believer, all the promises in the Bible are yours. As a Christian, we are to be Christ-like, demonstrating His characteristics. Our lives should take on newness; we should not think the same or act the same as in the past. When you know who you are in Christ, you're thinking becomes renewed to His Word (Romans 12:2). When you know who you are in Christ, you have the mind of Christ. (1 Corinthians 2:16)

As we learned in an earlier chapter the mind of Christ is having the same way of thinking that Jesus had. Jesus had a heart of love. He died on the cross an agonizing death so that we might have life abundantly (John 10:10). It is His will that all would be saved, not perish, and have everlasting life (John 3:16).

A few years ago, there was a show on MTV called *Real World.* The motto for *Real World* was, "When people stop being polite and start getting real." In order to fully live out the call of God in your life, you have to get real with yourself. You have to know who you truly are. In order to know who you truly are, you have to know who you are in Christ. You have to realize that God has a magnificent plan for your life.

I have found that getting real with yourself about your life's plan and purpose is fulfilling. Other people may not agree with how you lead your life, but as long as you are doing God's will, you are fine. One thing I have learned is this, you cannot expect people to support the dream and vision that God gave you. It is your dream and vision, guard it in your heart and mind.

When you know who you are in Christ, you will exude confidence. The opinions of people will no longer matter because you are living according to God's plan for your life.

Also, when you know who you are in Christ, you realize that your mission is greater than the obstacles before you. Remember, God is for you so who can be against you? (Romans 8:31)

Prayer

Prayer is simply a conversation with God. I have often heard people say, how do I pray? What do I pray? Think of talking to God as you would talk to a loving parent. In fact, God is our Father. God knows each and every one of our concerns. He knows the thoughts and the motives of the heart (Jeremiah 17:10). The Bible says to be anxious for nothing, and that through prayer we should make our requests known to God (Philippians 4:6) God is our Father, and He wants us to come to Him boldly. Just like our children have no hesitation in asking for what they want, as children of God, we have that same kind of access to God (Hebrews 4:16).

Prayer helps us to grow closer to God. Trust and believe God knows what we need and want. At the same time, He wants to hear from us. Prayer should be every day and continuous. The Bible says to pray without ceasing (1 Thessalonians 5:17) Praying without ceasing does not mean keeping your head bowed all day in prayer. In all things, in all decisions, seek God. I usually try to pray when I wake up in the morning and before I go to bed at night. Throughout the day, I talk to God in my mind. I may say, "Thank you God for another day. Thank you that my son is doing great. I thank you Lord that my students are turning into fine musicians!" Sometimes the things I say to God are so simple. I also pray for my family and friends. God honors His word and His word will never return void (Isaiah 55:11). Continue to pray knowing that God hears you. I believe prayer changes things. When you talk to God, be yourself. Please remember He already knows everything about you. He knows what you need before you even ask Him. Be as real and sincere as possible! Give thanks to the Lord, for He is good (Psalm 136).

I remember a time I prayed this prayer: "Jesus, help me to understand my life and the things that I am going through. You see the beginning and the end. You know the ins and outs. You see all the hidden details that I do not see. Order my steps. Help me to not stumble. Lead me to the right direction. Lead me to your path. Help me to not make the same mistakes. I want to do your will Jesus!"

I truly believe God heard my prayer. The Bible says that if we ask anything in His will, He hears us. (1 John 5:14) God's will is His Word. This is why it is so important to know God's word. How do you know what to ask if you do not know God's promises for you? Take small steps, you do not have to be a Bible scholar to talk to God. As I said before, God already knows your every need. Just pour your heart out to Him and watch God do a wonderful work in your life!

I recall one day having a great conversation with my friend, Sharmin Williams. She said as believers we need to pray big! We agreed that we would pray big prayers. Believe God for the extraordinary and miraculous in our lives! As believers we have to be bold with our faith. How do we expect unbelievers to become believers if we do not believe God for the extraordinary to happen in our lives? We are living epistles! We have dominion and authority based on the word of God! The Bible says that we shall decree a thing, and it shall come to pass! Remember, pray big!

As I said earlier, prayer is a big part of my life. I cannot go a day without talking to God in prayer. I can recollect a time I needed to pray to God on a serious matter. It was a few years ago, and I had suffered a heartbreaking miscarriage. I was devastated. My family and some of my friends knew I was pregnant. We were planning to have a shower, and the anticipation of a new baby in the family was exciting. Plus, this child would be my first child. I remember going to my obstetrician and she told me that I had a blighted ovum. There was no heartbeat, and she said the pregnancy would not progress. She recommended that I do a dilation and curettage. I was not hearing that. All I knew, is that I wanted my baby. I decided not to do the D&C, and proceeded to go home. I decided to wait and trust God to see what would happen.

During this time, I prayed. I remember being led to the story of Hannah in the Bible. Hannah wanted a baby and she could not get pregnant. So she sought God in prayer. She prayed that if God allowed her to get pregnant, she would dedicate her baby to God. Hannah eventually became pregnant, named her baby Samuel, and dedicated him to God. I decided to pray the prayer that Hannah prayed. I remember praying to God and telling Him that if he allowed me to get pregnant, I would dedicate my baby to Him.

About three weeks later, I had a natural miscarriage. The natural, physical pain was nothing compared to my emotional pain. I was deeply hurt and saddened by this. Even though, I had lost my baby, I decided not to give up hope on having a baby. After a few weeks later, my doctor cleared me to start trying to have a baby again. About two months later, I got pregnant again. I remember going to the doctor for my first visit. The sonogram showed a heartbeat! I indeed was truly pregnant. I remember the doctor saying what a strong heartbeat the baby had. I was overjoyed with tears streaming down my face. I remember thanking God profusely, for allowing me to get pregnant. And, as I had promised I dedicated my child to God. Throughout my pregnancy, I would read scriptures out loud to my baby. At 20 weeks of pregnancy, I found out I was having a boy. I was so excited! He was going to be the first boy in my family! My family was also very excited. I prayed to God to give me the name for him. I knew when I got pregnant, that I wanted my child to have a biblical name- whether it was a boy or a girl. God gave me the name Matthew. I named my son Matthew, which means "gift of God". He truly is heaven sent.   Also, throughout my pregnancy, I believed God kept giving me signs that I was to call my son Matthew. I remember driving and seeing various signs with the name Matthew. Also, when I watched TV, various characters would be named Matthew. I believe God was giving me signs everywhere! The ultimate sign, I believe happened two weeks before I delivered my baby boy. Matthew's father and I were in a store shopping for bedding. I was looking through the comforters, when a little child who looked about two years old, ran over my foot. His mom said, "Mateo don't do that!!" I started to laugh to myself. Mateo means Matthew in Spanish. At that point, I looked up, smiled, and said okay, Lord, I hear you. God always answers prayers. We are His children, and He wants to do good things for us (Psalm 103:5)

God is not limited by the things we see, meaning natural sources. Sometimes, we think that we are asking for something that God cannot deliver. You may say, how and can God do this? God is bigger than your problems and circumstances. The Bible says that His thoughts and ways are not our thoughts and ways. If it is within His will, God can and will do everything possible to allow your prayer to come to pass. If God has to move on the heart of someone to allow your prayer to happen, He will. I need you to understand that God is not limited by human limitations. He is El Shaddai, which means God Almighty. There is nothing too hard for our God, please believe that. Take the limits off of God, and you will see the limitless in your life. *The earth is the Lord's and the fullness thereof (*Psalm 24:1). My bible study teacher, Vivian Allen, once said when things are crazy in the natural that is when you go spiritual. Fasting is another spiritual concept.

Fasting

Along with prayer, comes fasting. Biblical fasting is abstaining from food for a period of time. I must say this, please seek advice from a medical doctor, especially if you have medical concerns. Some people fast for dietary or medical purposes. While on a fast, you voluntarily decide not to eat for a period of time. A fast can be for 24 hours, 3 days, 7 days, 21 days, or 40 days. I truly believe God will lead you in how much time you should fast. As a believer, we fast for spiritual reasons. Fasting is not only about you. You can go on a fast for other people. There have been plenty of times where people have fasted for loved ones. The period of abstaining from food, is the time you use to go in prayer to God. Fasting is for believers of all ages. Fasting is not a fad that comes and goes with the wind. It is biblical, and it is important spiritual tool. Fasting is not something that we broadcast and show off to the world. This is a personal and intimate act you do before God. The Bible does not say if we should fast, but when we fast. *"When you fast, do not look somber as the hypocrites do, for they disfigure their faces to show others they are fasting. Truly I tell you, they have received their reward in* full" (Matthew 6:16 NIV). There are plenty examples of people in the Bible who went on a fast and received a positive outcome. Think about Esther. She declared a fast and her people were spared from death. Also, Daniel fasted for 21 days and proved that the king's delicacies were not the choice food! Through Daniel's fast, he was able to bring people to

God who had not previously believed. Fasting is so that you can get a breakthrough in a particular area. We all need a breakthrough in some area of our lives. Fasting can turn a situation around. Jesus said, "The spirit is willing but the flesh is weak." (Matthew 26:41) Fasting can help to break addictions or certain temptations. Remember, the enemy comes to tempt us in three ways: through our eyes, our flesh, and the pride of life. Spiritual fasting helps to keep our flesh in submission to God's will. I truly believe fasting puts you in a position to receive a breakthrough. The breakthrough may come in different forms. Some people need a breakthrough in their finances, they go on a fast, and may receive a breakthrough in that area. Some people may fast to break a bad habit. Upon completion of a fast, they realize they no longer desire that habit. I believe fasting strengthens you, spiritually, physically and emotionally. I want to share some stories with you.

One of my dear friends is a believer and loves the Lord. She told me one day about her bad habit of smoking cigarettes. She knew that the Lord wanted her to quit smoking and that by doing so her health would significantly improve. She would smoke several cigarettes a day and was quite addicted to smoking, but she knew in order to live a long, healthy life and fulfill the call of God on her life, she would have to quit. So, she decided to go on a fast. When her fast was over, she realized she did not have the desire or need to smoke. Her cravings for smoking a cigarette vanished into thin air! It has been a year now and my friend is completely smoke-free!

I have another friend of mine who believed for her daughter to get a job. She shared how her daughter went on several job interviews, but with no success in getting a job. She decided to go on a fast for her daughter so that she would find employment. During this time, she lifted her daughter up in prayer with regards to getting a job. When her fast was complete, her daughter went on a job interview and was hired! Fasting works!

Another dear friend of mine felt that God was leading her into a season of fasting. She believed God wanted her to do a 40 day fast. She confided to me that she had never done a 40 day fast. She decided to do a Daniel Fast. During a Daniel Fast, you drink only water or 100% fruit juices. You do not consume sugar or sugar filled products. You eat mainly fruit, vegetables, and nuts. Another benefit of fasting is that it strengthens us. During this time, her faith in God increased. Her discernment became stronger. She had more clarity on spiritual matters. As she reflected back, she believed God was strengthening her for parent's transition. About two months later, after her fast, her parents went home to be with the Lord. As difficult as it was, she made it through. She attributes it to her period of prayer and fasting.

A friend of mine fasted for direction from God. She was at a crossroads in her life. She recently had lost her job and didn't know what to do. She wanted to move out of New York, but she was not sure if that was what God wanted her to do. She did not want to make any moves until she heard from God. My friend sought God in prayer and fasting. During this time, she felt led to fast for two weeks. Upon completion of her fast, she truly felt the Lord wanted her to move. A few months later she moved from NY and found a good paying job. She is now up for promotion!

Allow me to share another powerful testimony. Another friend of mine believed for her brother's salvation. She wanted her brother to know the Lord and have a relationship with him. For years, she prayed and prayed but to no avail. She had heard great testimonies from people who had fasted. She decided to go on a fast for her brother's salvation. She was led to go on a 7 day Daniel fast. Two weeks later, she invited her brother to go to church with her. Surprisingly, he went with her, considering he had not been to church in years. At the end of the service, they had an altar call. An altar call is when the pastor invites people to give their life to Christ; an open invitation to receive salvation. He accepted the invitation from the pastor and went up to the front of the church, along with other people. With tears streaming down her face, she watched as her brother gave his life to Christ. She truly believes it was due to her prayer and fasting that made this breakthrough happen. Some breakthroughs, I believe, will only happen when we go on a fast. *This kind does not go out except by prayer and fasting* (Matthew 17:21 AMP).

About two years ago, my Dad went to the doctor. During his visit, they discovered a cyst on his kidney. Automatically, I went into panic mode. I was like this cannot be. My spirit led me to pray. The doctors decided that they wanted to remove the kidney. When my parents told me about the cyst and the surgery, I decided to go on a fast. I was led to do a 7 day Daniel fast. During this time, my Dad went to the hospital. I continued to pray and fast. After my Dad's surgery, he recovered very well. And the cyst was benign. Praise God! I believe God heard my prayer.

Binding and Loosing (Spiritual Warfare)

"*I will give you the keys of the kingdom of heaven; whatever you bind on earth will be bound in heaven, and whatever you loose on earth will be loosed in heaven*" *(Matthew 16:19 NIV).* *"Behold! I have given you authority and power to trample upon serpents and scorpions, and [physical and mental strength and ability] over all the power that the enemy [possesses]; and nothing shall in any way harm you."* (Luke 10:19 AMP). As I stated earlier, we are triune in nature. We have a spirit, soul, and a body. Please understand there are spiritual forces at work, around us, demonic and angelic. We live in the natural realm, but there is also a spiritual realm. You may not see the spiritual realm with your natural eyes, but that does not mean it does not exist. As a believer, you are seated with Christ in heavenly places (Ephesians 2:6). This is not referring to heaven, the place that people go to when they die. This is a spiritual matter. This scripture means that we are above the spiritual forces, demonic as well as angelic. We have the authority to shift the atmosphere. We are able to do this with the words we speak.

Binding in the spiritual realm is tying a negative spirit. It is almost like a person who is handcuffed. When a person is handcuffed, they cannot move. So, it is in the spiritual realm as well. You cannot bind a person's free will, but you can bind the negative spirit within them. Whenever you bind up a negative spirit, this prevents the spirit from doing its work around you. As I stated earlier, we bind up spirits and negativity with our words. I will go more in depth on this in the next chapter. Here is a story of a person who used his words to bind up a negative spirit.

I have a friend who happens to be a car mechanic. He loves his work and enjoys working every day. The one thing he disliked was the negative atmosphere at the auto shop where he worked. He shared one time how the men would curse all day long and talk about negative and inappropriate topics. As a believer, he found it to be offensive. I spoke to him about binding and loosing. I asked him if he prayed about it. I also told him that before he goes into work, bind up the negative spirit in his workplace. He began to bind up the negativity with his words. In time, he began to see how the men were not cursing as much and the inappropriate talk ceased.

"Loosing" in the spiritual realm is the opposite of binding. Loosing is the act of releasing good benefits and blessings over you, other people, or a situation. We see a demonstration of this in Luke 13:12, *"And when Jesus saw her, he called her to him, and said unto her, Woman, thou art loosed from thine infirmity. And he laid his hands on her; and immediately she was made straight, and glorified God."* We see in this scripture, that Jesus first spoke a word, the spirit of sickness obeyed, and the woman was made whole. We are to follow the same example as Jesus. He has given us authority and dominion over the circumstances in our lives. Also, when we speak God's word we release angels to go to work on our behalf. *"The angel of the Lord encamps around those who fear him, and he delivers them."* (Psalm 34:7 NIV). *"Bless the Lord; you His angels, Who excel in strength, who do His word, Heeding the voice of His word."* (Psalm 103:20 NKJV). We can *shift the atmosphere* by the words we speak.

Let me share a story about the act of "loosing" with you. My friend's mother had been on dialysis for several years. She believed that God would send her a donor match and receive a kidney. Day in and day out, she prayed with unwavering faith. She began to speak in the affirmative. She would say I thank you God for my kidney, thank you Lord for sending me a donor. She would speak this even though, she had not received a kidney, and there was not a donor in sight! One day while receiving her dialysis treatment, a hospital contacted her dialysis center about the availability of a kidney. At once, she had to leave to receiver her new organ! A few hours later, her surgery was successful and she had her kidney. She no longer had to endure painful dialysis treatments. She was indeed made whole! She attributes this to her faith in God and speaking in the affirmative that her kidney was here. Words are truly powerful. You can bring life or death to a situation by the words you speak.

Keys to Remember

- We are triune in nature- spirit, soul, and body
- God has given us authority over the works of the enemy
- Authority means power
- As a believer, we have the mind of Christ
- The mind of Christ is the thinking of Christ
- God's promises are for all believers
- Prayer is a conversation with God
- Prayer draws us near to God

- Prayer works
- Fasting improves our discernment
- Fasting can turn a situation around
- There are two realms- natural & spiritual

- Binding is tying up a demonic or negative spirit
- Loosing is releasing blessings over a person or situation
- We bind and loose with our words

Chapter 6

SPEAK LIFE

Death and life are in the power of the tongue: and they that love it shall eat the fruit thereof. ~ Proverbs 18:21

Did you know that the words you say can produce success or failure in your life? The Bible says that death and life is in the power of the tongue. This means that whatever you say will bring either death or life to your circumstances. Our words create the world around us. If you are failing or not having success in an area in your life, check what you are saying. Often, we speak about our problems rather than speak to the problem. You are the prophet of your life. You can prophesy death or life to a situation. Your current situation is a manifestation of what you have been thinking and saying. Your tongue is your most powerful asset. *Likewise, the tongue is a small part of the body, but it makes great boasts. Consider what a great forest is set on fire by a small spark* (James 3:5 NIV). Your words carry the power to change any situation. You need to hold in respectful regard the words you speak. You can smite yourself with your own words or you can live an overcoming, victorious life. Be aware of the words you speak and also the words you speak over others.

As I previously stated, your words have power. The things that we speak are creating the future we will see. As you speak, your words are lining up to bring what you say to pass. As people of God, we need to stop speaking negative situations and circumstances over our lives. Stop communicating fear and speak faith-filled words.

As a believer, we know that God created the world with His word. God thought it, spoke it, and then saw what He said. We need to do the same. Think and speak according to God's word. With this action, we will see the

85

manifestation of the things we are believing. If you want success in your life, speak success. If you want health and wealth, speak it over your life. It is God's will for you to have these things. *Beloved, I pray that you may prosper in all things and be in health, just as your soul prospers* (3 John 1:2). When you are a believer, circumstances do not have control over you, you control the circumstances. You can shift and change what is around you, by the words you speak. Communicate with words that edify and magnify. God did not give us fear, but a spirit of love, power, and a sound mind. Exercise your authority! The Bible instructs us in Romans 4:17 to call those things that be not as though they are. "*As it is written, I have made you the father of many nations. "[He was appointed our father] in the sight of God in Whom he believed, Who gives life to the dead and speaks of the nonexistent things that [He has foretold and promised] as if they [already] existed.*" (Romans 4:17 AMP). Often, we speak what we see in the natural, which is usually negative, instead of speaking what we want to see. Always speak in the affirmative based on God's word.

I remember one day I was at work, and a coworker of mine was complaining. Sadly to say, she often complained. I noticed many things she said were negative. She always had an issue with something. She griped about hating the job and even some of the people. She felt she did not get paid enough. I am an encourager, so I would always try to encourage. I told her to not say negative things and start to look at having a job as a blessing. There are many who are looking for work and would gladly have her job. The more negative she spoke, the more negative her situation became.

A friend of mine who I love dearly, would always verbalize her fear of car accidents. She would say things like, "I'm scared to drive, and driving on the road is scary." She would emphasize her fear of driving time and again. I felt like she gave her fear of driving life. The amazing and sad thing is that for the past 4 years she has had an accident *every* year! Words have power! You will have what you say!

A dear friend of mine would complain about his lack of money. Even though he was working he always verbalized how he did not have enough money. At times he felt he was barely getting by. He would often say, "I just want to be comfortable. I don't need to be wealthy, just comfortable." I would listen to him as he made these self-defeating statements. I would try to encourage him and tell him things would get better. One day, it dawned on me the words he was uttering. I realized the Bible says death and life is in the power of the tongue. You will have what you say. I believe the reasons he could not get out of that financial rut was because of the words he was saying. He always said he wanted to be comfortable and that was the lifestyle he was living, just enough. I told him stop saying you want to be comfortable. I do not believe God wants us to live comfortable. Why, because in John 10:10, Jesus said that He came so that we can live life abundantly. Therefore, our aim should be to live in abundance. If we live in abundance, we can be a blessing to others. You cannot live in lack and bless others simultaneously. Abundance means overflow and more than enough. I speak abundance over my own life and family, too. We are blessed to be a blessing. I want to be able to bless others without feeling like I cannot do it due to lack of funds. I have declared over my own life that I want supernatural results! I want to live an extraordinary not an ordinary life!

The Power of Agreement

"Can two walk together, unless they are agreed?" (Amos 3:3 NKJV) In everyday life, we experience the power of agreement on various matters. For example, the other day a coworker of mine invited my son and me to a play date. We discussed where we would meet and the time. We agreed that it would be great for the

children to play while we chatted for a few hours. We made a final agreement. When you schedule a doctor's visit, you call and make an appointment. You and your doctor agree on the time, and the agreement is that your doctor will be there to tend to your needs.   In biblical terms, the power of agreement is getting into agreement with another believer on God's word about a particular situation. *Again I say to you that if two of you agree on earth concerning anything that they ask, it will be done for them by My Father in heaven. "For where two or three are gathered together in My name, I am there in the midst of them."* (Matthew 18:19-20 NKJV).   A friend of mine was concerned because her son was going to college and she wanted him to receive scholarships and grants. We prayed in agreement that her son would receive the necessary funding for school. About two months later, he received scholarship money and she only had to pay for his books for the year! Another friend of mine, believed for a child and after several failed attempts at conceiving, she felt hopeless but still wanted a child. While at a prayer meeting, the mothers in the room, decided to pray in agreement, that God would open her womb to receive conception. The praise report is that a year later, she gave birth to a beautiful, healthy son! One of my friends had believed God for a car, but she did not have the finances at the time to get one. Her son, who is of great faith, told his mother that he wanted to pray in agreement for a car. His faith was unwavering. Several months later, she bought a car, with very low monthly payments. What you need to understand is that God's word never fails, never loses its power, and never returns void!! It is not a matter of if the Word works, but when the Word works. A very good friend of mine is a successful musician. He has worked with some very great artists and goes on tour around the country regularly. He is a working musician! I told him it is also my desire to go on tour and

91

perform as well. I told him how passionate I was about my playing the flute. He said to me, "Your time is coming. You will be doing the same thing, watch and see!" I was overjoyed instantly, and said, "Yes, I agree!" Now, I'm waiting for the manifestation. I believe God will deliver. The power of agreement can also work in the negative. Sometimes, people will speak negative words into the atmosphere, and if you agree, the very thing you do not want to show up in your life, will. This is why it is so important to think about the things you are speaking. I recall one time I was at a party, and one of my friends said to me, "I see your sister is traveling abroad. Are you planning to travel abroad?" Another person chimed in and said, "Dara, please she's not going anywhere!" She figured she would make the group laugh. The few of them chuckled a bit. I said, "Not now, but I will. It's not the time for it." Now, this may seem like a simple, mundane, harmless conversation, but for where I am believing God to take me, I cannot take on idle words over my life. I am going after the greater and latter rain!!! *"Most assuredly, I say to you, he who believes in Me, the works that I do he will do also; and greater works than these he will do, because I go to My Father."* (John 14:12 NKJV).

Be Conscious of Your Words

I am fully aware of the words I speak. I make a conscious effort not to speak negative words. I also, do not come into agreement when people speak negative. I recall a time I was at work and some people were saying how expensive everything was as they complained about their lack of money. I remember one person saying, "I'm always broke, and I will stay broke." I felt like someone had punched me in the stomach. Those words almost sent me into a shock. In my mind, I was thinking, no, do not say that. I remember even saying to her, "Do you want to stay broke? Do you like not having money? Is living check to check decent enough for you?" Of course she replied no.

Then I proceeded to tell her that her words have power. I encouraged her to be more aware of the words she spoke. I truly believe when we align our words with God's word, we have the power to turn around a situation. Speak the right words, and the right things will follow. Speak words that edify, words that strengthen, and words that increase. Do not speak of what you see, speak what you want to see. Speak as if what you want is already here. The Bible instructs us that we are to *call those things that be not as though they are* (Romans 4:17). Do not speak about your problems, speak to your problems. *For assuredly, I say to you, whoever says to this mountain, "Be removed and be cast into the sea", and does not doubt in his heart, but believes that those things he says will be done, he will have whatever he says* (Mark 11:23 NKJV). Often, I find we are not speaking the right words, because we are not thinking the right thoughts.

Think the Right Thoughts

Thoughts are ideas, concepts, or images in a person's mind. The power to think is a gift from God and we are free to choose how we think. Our thoughts affect our attitudes and behavior. In order to speak the right words, we have to know what to think. Our thinking needs to come from the word of God. The Bible gives us a compass on what to think. *Finally, brethren, whatsoever things are true, whatsoever things are honest, whatsoever things are just, whatsoever things are pure, whatsoever things are lovely, whatsoever things are of good report; if there be any virtue, and if there be any praise, think on these things* (Philippians 4:8). We have to think thoughts in align with who and what God says we are. We cannot go around speaking negatively, and expect a positive outcome. This is why the scripture tells us to meditate and think on positive things. You cannot have a negative mindset and expect to live a positive life. It does not work that way. A negative mindset will prevent you from living out your full purpose. There are several things you must understand about thoughts. Thoughts are powerful. *"What you decide on will be done, and light will shine on your ways"* (Job 22:28 NIV) Thoughts become things. *"For as he thinketh in his heart, so is he."* (Proverbs 23:7) Get your thinking from the word of God. It is important to guard your thoughts. *"We demolish arguments and every pretension that sets itself up against the knowledge of God, and we take captive every thought to make it obedient to Christ."* (2 Corinthians 10:5 NIV). Confess the Word daily. Speak the Word daily and watch God change your circumstances and life. *"That person is like a tree planted by streams of water, which yields its fruit in season and whose leaf does not wither- whatever they do prospers."* (Psalm 1:3 NIV).

Speak God's Word

There are several things you need to know about God's Word. His Word is eternal. *Heaven and earth shall pass away, but my words shall not pass away* (Matthew 24:35). God's Word does not return void. *So shall My word be that goes forth from My mouth; It shall not return to Me void, But it shall accomplish what I please, And it shall prosper in the thing for which I sent it* (Isaiah 55:11 NKJV). God watches over His Word. *The Lord said to me, "You have seen correctly, for I am watching to see that my word is fulfilled* (Jeremiah 1:12). Angels go to work on your behalf when the Word is spoken. *"Bless the Lord, you His angels, Who excel in strength, who do His word, Heeding the voice of His word."* (Psalm 103:20 NKJV). God's word is His will. *Now this is the confidence that we have in Him, that if we ask anything according to His will, He hears us. And if we know that He hears us, whatever we ask, we know that we have the petitions that we have asked of Him* (1 John 5:14-15).

When you speak God's Word, know that He hears you, and His word will not return void. In order to speak God's word, you have to know what He says in His scriptures. I suggest committing scriptures to memory. Think of a situation you need a breakthrough in, and research scriptures based on that topic. For example, if you are in need of healing. You will look for healing scriptures. Here are some examples. *"Beloved, I pray that you may prosper in all things and be in health, just as your soul prospers."* (3 John 1:2 NKJV). *"Bless the Lord, O my soul; And all that is within me, bless His holy name! Bless the Lord, O my soul, And forget not all His benefits: Who forgives all your iniquities, Who heals all your diseases."* (Psalm 103:1-3 NKJV). If you are in need of a financial breakthrough, you will speak scriptures based on finances over your situation. *"And my God shall supply all your need according to His* riches in glory in Christ Jesus." (Philippians 4:19 NKJV). "And you shall remember the Lord your God, for it is He who gives you power to get wealth that He may establish His covenant which He swore to your fathers, as it is this day." (Deuteronomy 8:18 NKJV). If you are feeling discouraged, you will need scriptures to encourage you. "Trust in the Lord with all your heart, And lean not on your own understanding; In all your ways acknowledge Him, and He shall direct your paths." (Proverbs 3:5-6). "Peace I leave with you, My peace I give to you; not as the world gives do I give to you. Let not your heart be troubled, neither let it be afraid." (John 14:27 NKJV). If you are in need of divine protection, you speak scriptures to enlist heavenly protection. I personally love Psalm 91. It is a powerful protection Psalm, I pray it every night before I go to bed. "I will say of the Lord, He is my refuge and my fortress; My God, in Him I will trust" (Psalm 91:2 NKJV). As I said earlier, research scriptures that deal with your situation and begin to speak them over your life. I suggest memorizing the scripture. However, I strongly urge you to meditate on the scripture. Meditating on a scripture is allowing a scripture to get deep rooted within. You may say that scripture repeatedly until it becomes a reality in your life.

God's Word Has Power

Dear friends, you must realize that God's word has power. His Word has the power to transform you. *"For the Word that God speaks is alive and full of power [making it active, operative, energizing, and effective]; it is sharper than any two-edged sword, penetrating to the dividing line of the breath of life (soul) and [the immortal] spirit, and of joints and marrow [of the deepest parts of our nature], exposing and sifting and analyzing and judging the very thoughts and purposes of the heart."* (Hebrews 4:12 AMP). *"And do not be conformed to this world, but be transformed by the renewing of* your mind, that you may prove what is that good and acceptable and perfect will of God." (Romans 12:2 NKJV). God's word has the power to bring faith. "So then faith comes by hearing, and hearing by the word of God." (Romans 10:17 NKJV). God's Word has the power to heal. "Then they cried out to the Lord in their trouble, And He saved them out of their distresses. "He sent His word and healed them, And delivered them from their destructions." (Psalm 107:19-20 NKJV). God's Word has the power to bring prosperity. "And my God shall supply all your need according to His riches in glory by Christ Jesus." (Philippians 4:19 NKJV). God's word has the power to fight the enemy. "When evening had come, they brought to Him many who were demon-possessed. And He cast out the spirits with a word, and healed all who were sick, that it might be fulfilled which was spoken by Isaiah the prophet, saying: "He Himself took our infirmities And bore our sicknesses." (Matthew 8:16 NKJV).

Based on God's Word declare who you are. I suggest you write down affirmations about yourself. Then begin to read them aloud daily. As you read the words, let them take root deep down in your spirit. Allow God's word to penetrate your heart and mind. Allow the truth of His word to transform your thinking, and you will begin to see the manifestation of His word in your life.   Here are some affirmations that I say over my own life.

Affirmations Based on God's Word

- I am the head, not the tail (Deuteronomy 28:13)
- I am above not beneath (Deuteronomy 28:13)
- I am fearfully and wonderfully made (Psalm 139:14)
- God has a great plan for me (Jeremiah 29:11)
- I live an abundant life (John 10:10)
- Wealth and riches are in my house (Psalm 112:3)

- I am healthy (3 John 1:2)

- I do not fear because I have power, love, and a sound mind (2 Timothy 1:7)

- I am blessed and highly favored (Luke 1:28)

- I will see the goodness of the Lord in the land of the living (Psalm 27:13)

- I am daily loaded with benefits (Psalm 68:19)

- I am wealthy (Deuteronomy 8:18)

- My son loves the Lord (Proverbs 22:6)

- My life is crowned with favor (Psalm 5:12)

- I will live a long life (Psalm 91:16)

- Angels encamp around myself and my family (Psalm 34:7)

- I am humble, therefore God will exalt me (Matthew 23:12)

- I have favor with God and with man (Proverbs 3:4)

- I cast my cares on the Lord because He cares for me (1 Peter 5:7)

- I am a new creature in Christ (2 Corinthians 5:17)
- I think positive thoughts (Proverbs 23:7)
- No weapon formed against me or my family shall prosper (Isaiah 54:17)
- I am debt free (Romans 13:8)
- I am a doer of the Word (James 1:22)
- I am blessed by the works of my hands (Deuteronomy 2:7)

Keys to Remember

- Pray and meditate on God's word daily
- Learn to think based on God's word
- Learn to believe based on God's word
- Learn to say things in alignment with God's word
- Speak God's word daily
- Study the Word of God
- Find scriptures based on your situation to meditate on
- God watches over His word to perform it
- Angels go to work on your behalf when the Word is spoken
- God's word never returns void

Chapter 7

KNOW NO LIMITS

"Now to Him Who, by (in consequence of) the [action of His] power that is at work within us, is able to [carry out His purpose and] do superabundantly, far over and above all that we [dare] ask or think [infinitely beyond our highest prayers, desires, thoughts, hopes, or dreams]"
(Ephesians 3:20 AMP)

The Bible says to not cast away your confidence, for there is a great recompense of reward (Hebrews 10:35). This chapter is for those who have hopes and dreams. If you have a dream that is so great that in the natural seems impossible, know that it is possible with God. God says that with Him all things are possible. What seems insurmountable to man is a walk in the park for God. My dreams are so much greater than me that I need God to move on my behalf in order for them to come to pass. In the Word it says, *"If God is for us, who can be against us."* (Romans 8:31) God wants your dreams to come to pass. If you have a dream that will not go away, it is there because God put it there. Often, I hear people say I am waiting on God, when God is actually waiting on you. He is waiting to hear what you are going to say about your situation. If you speak success, you will succeed. On the other hand, if you speak failure, you will fail.

There is a common saying: "sick and tired of being sick and tired." There has to come a point in one's life, when enough is enough. Why do we settle for less, when God is ready, willing and able to give us so much more? In my own life, I have determined and resolved within my spirit that I am going to go after all that Christ died to give me. Jesus said that He came to give us life abundantly.

Abundance encompasses everything from health, wealth, family, and every other area of life. So many people are just living day to day and not really enjoying their life. God does not want us to merely exist. He wants us to live an enriched life! The Word says *"Delight yourself in Him, and He will give you the desires of your heart"* (Psalm 37:4).

Tyrese Gibson, a famous musician, actor, and author once said, "The only limits that are created are the ones that you create for yourself!" That's pretty deep. We can be our own worst enemy at times. We halt our own progress, through our mindset and unbelief. You have to come to a point in life that you want a change and move forward to make it so. God created us to live abundantly, therefore, go after every God given dream and goal! All things are possible when your belief lines up with God's way of thinking. When this happens, you will live a life without limits. God is not limited by your upbringing, education, or where you come from. God is not limited by our natural circumstances. Remember, God is omniscient. He knows *everything*. God is the Alpha and the Omega. He knows every step and detail of your life! I have found that often our decisions and choices that we make are a reflection of various aspects in our lives. There are several factors that hinder or encourage our push for no limits. Some factors are our upbringing, how we were raised, and the family dynamics in the home that we grew up in. Others are our school experiences, whether positive or negative, both can have an effect on your thinking. Other factors, such as friends, church, or social activities can play a great part in our belief system. To have no limits, you have to first believe that there are *no limits*! One of the first mandates that God gave mankind was to have dominion and authority. As we learned in a previous chapter, dominion means to have control over, and authority means power. *"And God blessed them and said to them, Be fruitful, multiply, and fill the earth, and subdue it [using all its vast resources in the service of God and man]; and have dominion over the fish of the sea, the birds of the air, and over every living creature that moves upon the earth."* (Genesis 1:28 AMP).

Quentin J. Rogers, an entrepreneur, said, "Dreams are not practical jokes played on us. They are seeds sown in our hearts that are meant for us to water with the right mindset, cultivate with the right connections, and help grow through action. Wake up and start living your dream." I have realized that often the dreams and vision that God gave us will require us to push past our limits and get into the zone of no limitations. I believe if we really understood the dominion and authority that God gave us, we would live limitless. We would stop the negative self-talk and like a super hero, conquer over our circumstances. Please understand, knowing no limits is taking a risk. Your friends and family may ridicule you for pushing towards the limitless life, and that is okay. This is your vision, your dream, your ambition, your goals for your life. You may have dreams that are so big, that if you were to tell someone, they may think you are crazy! I say step out on faith! I truly believe God gives us dreams that are bigger than ourselves, and we need to trust Him in order for it to come to pass. God knows the right people. The right breaks, the open doors, and everything else you need to fulfill your destiny! Don't give up! Keep pressing forward!

As I said earlier, our past experiences often will dictate how we view the world around us. One day, I was having an interesting conversation with a business associate of mine, he said, "The majority of people are programmed to settle for less from childhood. So of course, they will doubt your great vision. Keep striving!" I remember growing up, my Mom and Dad were always very supportive of me. They encouraged me in my various interests. They always tried to push me to do the best that I could. While they had similar views on raising me, I observed that they were different in some ways. My mom liked to play it safe and was not much of a risk taker. She would not do something out of the ordinary. I recall when I first told her about *Dara Marie Productions*, she looked shocked and almost worried. Her first question, "How are you going to do that and your job at the same time? You know jobs are good, they are stable. Plus, you're a teacher, you get a good pension, you're tenured" and on and on she went. Now, mind you, I did not tell her that I was quitting my job and moving forward with this project full force. I decided I would work it in tandem with my job. I remember, telling my Dad for the first time about *Dara Marie Productions,* and his reaction was quite different. He said, "Wow! That's great! Give it a shot; you never know what will happen! I wish you the best!" Notice, how *different* both reactions were. I learned a very interesting lesson that day. I learned that your mindset has everything to do with what you will and won't do! I also learned that people's life experiences affect how they react and navigate in the world.

My mom was born in New York. She grew up in a middle-class household where she was taught go to school, get an education, and get a good job. And, while I believe education is important, having several degrees myself, I do not believe that it is the only route to success. I am truly thankful to my parents because without them I probably would not have an education. My father grew up poor in Jamaica. On April 25, 1967, my Dad came to the United States of America and began a new life. He came here alone with no family, no friends, and only a few dollars in his pocket. Through many ups and downs he persevered and never gave up. He worked several jobs as a waiter then eventually put himself through school and ended up working at Con Edison.

When I reflect back on his life, it takes a lot of courage to leave a country you're familiar with and to move to another country that is strange territory. It takes courage, perseverance, and dedication, to keep moving forward and not give up. One day, I remember asking him why came to the United States. He said for a better life, and he knew that the opportunities here were limitless; that you succeed if you really wanted to. From watching my Dad, I learned the power of persistence and courage. If you want to live a life without limits, you will have to step out on faith, take a risk, and forge ahead! Steve Harvey, a successful comedian and talk show host, once said, "If you want to be successful, you have to jump. You have to take a leap of faith!" You will never get past comfortable, if you always do what is comfortable. Take risks. You will never know what you are made of unless you push yourself out of your comfort zone. You cannot do things the way you have always done them, and expect things to turn out differently. To get a different result, you have to take a different course of action. Know no limits!

The Power of Perseverance

According to Merriam-Webster's Dictionary, perseverance means, "continued effort to do or achieve something despite difficulties, failure or opposition." In spite of obstacles, perseverance means don't give up, don't quit, and don't throw in the towel. Please understand, as long as you are alive, obstacles and challenges will present themselves, but you still have to remain steadfast and keep pushing toward living a limitless life.

I also need to encourage you to not stay stuck on suffering. Unfair things will happen in life, but you have to stay focused on moving forward! Life happens, but in the midst of it you have to trust God. Stop replaying the bad things that happened to you in your mind. Yes, life can be challenging, but you will get through it. In order for you to be happy and live the limitless life, you have to do the work. You have to keep trudging forward, don't give up! Think about what is good in your life and move on! Like a CD player, some people have the bad things that happened to them on repeat. I say press forward, and move on to the next song! Remember, God knows everything about you, and I truly believe better days are ahead if you will persevere.

When I think about the power of perseverance, I am reminded of Job. In the Bible, Job endured tragedy after tragedy. At one point, his wife encouraged him to give up his faith on God. *Then his wife said to him, "Do you still hold fast to your integrity? Curse God and die!"* (Job 2:9NKJV). In spite of all he had endured, Job persevered and never quit believing. There are several things that can be learned from this. **You can choose to accept**

the past. *"Brethren, I do not count myself to have apprehended; but one thing I do, forgetting those things which are behind and reaching forward to those things which are ahead, I press toward the goal for the prize of the upward call of God in Christ Jesus."* (Philippians 3:13-14 NKJV). **You can choose to embrace the present.** *"And we know that all things work together for good to those who love God, to those who are the called according to His purpose."* (Romans 8:28 NKJV). **You can look expectantly toward the future.** *"For I know the plans I have for you, declares the Lord, plans to prosper you and not to harm you, plans to give you hope and a future."* (Jeremiah 29:11 NIV). Remember, God is always at work on your behalf. Keep persevering and live a life without limits!

The Power of Patience

According to Merriam-Webster's Dictionary, patience means, "the capacity, habit, or fact of being patient." On Vocabulary.com, it says that patience, "is a person's ability to wait something out or endure something tedious, without getting riled up." Often, when we are in the state of waiting we may become anxious, frustrated, or even angry. Now, keep in mind while you are in the state of waiting for a vision to come to pass which will elevate you to the limitless life, you must demonstrate patience. Here are several things that you can do while you are waiting and being patient. **Encourage yourself.** Many times we are looking for external sources to keep us happy and motivated and to help us push past our limitations. The Bible says how David encouraged himself in the Lord (1 Samuel 30). Reflect on past things that God has done for you. Believe that if He did it for you once, He will do it again. *Wait for the Lord; be strong and take heart and wait for the Lord* (Psalm 27:14 NIV). **Serve God.** Jesus said He was about His Father's business (Luke 2:49). Be diligent in doing the things the Lord has called you to do. By doing these things, you will get closer to God and also renew your strength. **Know God's promises.** Meditate on God's word. Study the Bible. Know the promises of God that you are standing on for your particular situation. *Delight yourself also in the Lord, and He shall give you the desires of your heart* (Psalm 37:4 NKJV). **Rest in God's character.** God does not compromise or change His values. *But the Lord's plans stand firm forever; his intentions can never be shaken* (Psalm 33:11 NLT). **Rely on God's love.** God said that He would never leave us or forsake us. He says that He loves us with an everlasting love (Jeremiah 31:3). **Seek God's face.** By seeking God's face, you will have a deeper relationship with God. This is an ongoing daily process that needs to happen in your life. *As the deer pants for the water brooks, so pants my soul for You, O God* (Psalm 42:1 NKJV). **Walk uprightly.** This is not a time for shortcuts. Be patient and keep persevering. Be obedient in the things God has called you to do. *For the Lord God is a sun and shield; The Lord will give grace and glory; no good thing will He withhold from those who walk uprightly* (Psalm 84:11 NKJV).

Small Strides

And let us not be weary in well doing: for in due season we shall reap, if we faint not (Galatians 6:9). As I said earlier, living the limitless life will require doing that which makes you uncomfortable. You cannot stay in your comfort zone and expect to grow. Take small strides. Let me share a story with you. This may sound funny. When I would go to get a pedicure, I would always choose a shade of pink. I never veered from that color. It did not matter what shade it was, as long as it was pink! I never ventured and tried other colors like blue or green, because in my mind, I didn't think it was conservative or appropriate to wear to work. So one day, I decided to take the limits off, and try a different color! I remember trying a shade of blue. As funny as it sounds, I told myself to be brave and try a different color for my manicure and pedicure. I think sometimes in order to step out of the box, it will require small strides. Take small increasing steps each day, push yourself! And remember, no limits!

This is Your Life

Please understand, you are given one life and your life is your responsibility. If you are waiting on someone else to create the life you want, you will be waiting forever! You cannot wait on someone else to make changes for you. Only you can create the life you want! Do not put your life on hold for someone else. This is the only life you have that God gave you. You must decide what you want and do not want, and only you can make that decision. Yes, God will bring people that can influence you and push you to your purpose. God will also put people around you that will elevate and motivate you, but ultimately it will be you who puts ideas to action. No one is going to force you to live your best life! You have to want it bad enough for it to happen. Connect with other people who believe in your vision. Awaken your imagination to the possibilities in your life. What is your deepest desire? What do you truly want to accomplish during your lifetime? How do you want to be remembered? Be free from people's opinions. People opinions cannot help you. I often ask, "Why do we live our lives through the lens of someone else?" They are not walking in your shoes, you are! You also have to know when to keep your mouth shut. You cannot share your dreams and goals with everyone. Everybody is not going to celebrate with you. Beware of the naysayers! Keep speaking to God about your hopes and dreams. As God elevates you, remember to stay humble! Also, food for thought, do not allow other people who do not have enough faith for their own life or situations they are going through, speak into your life. Be very stringent about the criteria in which you allow other people to speak into your life. Remember, words have power! When it comes to your dreams, you have to have tunnel vision. Determine to be unstoppable and pursue that dream that is within you.

Go After It

I have decided that I am not going to quit. I am not going to fail. I will succeed. I will "go in" on life! God gave me the gift of life, and He also gave you the gift of life. You need to pursue your purpose. Go after every God given dream, goal, and vision. Everything that God has downloaded and put into your heart and spirit, GO AFTER IT! Be relentless! Don't quit! Go after your dreams as if your life depends on it! Do not sway to the left or right! Focus on your dreams and goals! No distractions! Do not be concerned about other people's opinions. They are not walking in your shoes! God did not give them the dream, He gave it to you. God trusts you to go after the vision. Evangelist Wendy Key once said, "You don't have to explain to anyone your next move in life. People will not always understand where God is taking you. Often times, telling your dreams, goals, and aspirations will get you put in the pit, just like Joseph." I urge you to keep pushing past the limitations until it becomes a reality.

The Bible says that, "until now the kingdom of heaven suffers violence, and the violent take it by force" (Matthew 11:12). You have to take it by force! Success is not going to just fall in your lap! In order to be successful, you're going to have to go after it every day. As I said earlier, you will have to be relentless and tenacious in your focus to see and accomplish the limitless life. You have to be determined and persistent to know no limits.

At this point, quitting is not an option. You cannot compromise your vision. You cannot say, "Oh, well," if it does not happen. There is only one plan. And that is to succeed. Like a track star, jump over the hurdles and keep going. Keep pressing and pushing past the limits. Know no limits!

Keys to Remember

- With God all things are possible
- God wants your dreams to come to pass
- God wants you to live an abundant life
- When we delight in God, He gives us the desires of our hearts
- Pursue every God-given dream
- God is not limited by our natural circumstances
- Your life is your responsibility
- Having patience and perseverance is key to living the limitless life
- Living the limitless life requires courage, dedication, and persistence
- Quitting is not an option

Chapter 8

DEMONSTRATING EXCELLENCE

"And whatever you do, do it heartily, as to the Lord and not to men, knowing that from the Lord you will receive the reward of the inheritance; for you serve the Lord Christ"
(Colossians 3:23-24 NKJV)

We are ambassadors of Christ; therefore, we are to strive for excellence in everything that we do. Non-Christians are watching to see if this Jesus that we speak of is real, and if He is making a difference in our lives. I remember once reading a quote that said, "The only Bible people may read is you". The Bible instructs us, *to let our light shine before others that they may see our good works and glorify our Father in heaven* (Matthew 5:16). Excellence is something that honors

God. Jesus died so that we could live the abundant life. When we strive to excel, we honor the promise that Jesus gave us about abundant life. Mediocrity does not honor God. Mediocrity is doing just enough to get by, it is barely enough; it is less than excellent service. In order to do everything in an excellent manner, you have to set your mind to achieve greatness.

Spending Time with God

I believe in order to know what we are called to do, and in order to do it excellently, we need to spend time with God. As I said earlier, God created us; He knows our entire life story. *And there is no creature hidden from His sight, but all things are naked and open to the eyes of Him to whom we must give account* (Hebrews 4:13 NKJV). We need to pray to God, and He will reveal to us the plan on how to proceed in the things that concern us. I truly believe God gives us insight and a strategy on how to do everything with excellence. Every day, I try to set aside time to spend with God. This is my quiet and alone time with God. I will pray to Him, tell Him my concerns, and the desires of my heart. I will also praise Him for what He's done, what He's doing, and what He will do! God is so faithful. He desires to spend time with His people. I believe the many heartaches and setbacks we've had is because we haven't spent enough time with God and listen to His will for our lives. When we spend time with God, He will download and reveal His plan for our lives. I also suggest reading your Bible. Read a little each day. You may not read lengthily chapters daily, but make an effort to read God's Word. I believe God will honor and reward your faithfulness in spending time with Him.

One of my friends is in ministry, and I asked her how she knew that God called her into ministry. She told me through spending time with God that is how she received clarification. She said as Christians our first call is to God. She said did not make any moves into ministry until she had the conversation with God. God will tell you what you need to do. Sometimes, we try to bypass God and take a shortcut. That is when we fall in error. God is orderly; He does not do things haphazardly. He is not the author of confusion (1 Corinthians 14:33). She said that God called her for a season. The calling was to come into His presence. My dear friend confided that she prayed and fasted for quite some time. After this, then God released her into ministry. That was the commission. She said many times we as people try to move ahead or too quickly before God's timing. His timing may not be our timing, although He is right on time. She said spending time with God allowed her to not have any missteps. She was moving in perfect synchronization with what He planned for her.

The ultimate example of spending time with God is Jesus. Jesus had to wait 30 years before He began His ministry. Before this time,

129

He had spent plenty of time with God. He knew from young that He was the Messiah and God had commissioned Him to be the Savior of the world. He had to wait for God's perfect timing to be released. Spending time with God puts everything in perspective. When you spend time with God, He will show you how to go about do everything with excellence.

Excellence requires Commitment

There are several things I am passionate about, and one of them is of course, music. I have played the flute since I was eight years old. As I got older, I realized that I wanted music to be a major part of my life. In high school, I remember practicing for hours in my parents' basement. I would practice into the wee hours of the morning. I did this because I was committed to playing the flute, and I thoroughly enjoyed it. At the age of 16, when everyone else I knew was having Sweet 16 parties, I decided that I did not want one. I remember telling my parents, I do not want a

Sweet 16 party, but I want a really good flute, and I want private flute lessons. My parents were like, "Wow! She's serious about this." At that point, my parents realized I was committed to playing the flute and developing my craft further. Commitment requires being all in or dedicated to a cause. When you are committed to something, you will see it to its fruition and realization.

I have been an elementary band director for the past 16 years. In all the years I have taught band, I have had students that were committed to playing their instrument. I must say, I have one student in particular that comes to mind. When I say commitment, she as a young student epitomizes what it means to be fully committed. I had the pleasure of teaching her the clarinet for the past 3 years. Recently, she has moved on to the junior high school band. She is the kind of student that I would have to teach her a concept one time and that was it. I recall a time that she wanted to skip her physical education class so that she could have a longer music lesson! What child wants to skip physical education? I do not know many children who would. She would go home and practice for hours. Keep in mind she is only 11 years old. She told me that she would practice during the week, Monday through Friday, for 2 hours a day! And the only reason she did not practice more than that was because of her homework.   On the weekend, she would practice for 6 to 7 hours. This student is a fully committed student, and I know she will go very far in her gift of playing the clarinet! She is exceptionally faithful! It was an honor to be her teacher; she showed me the power of commitment. Everything she did was saturated with excellence! She excelled in all of her subjects and truly dedicated to being outstanding.

People that are extremely committed run the risk of people saying that they are overzealous. In order to do something in an excellent manner, you must be committed. When you are committed to excellence, you will see a project through until completion. Recently, I watched the movie "Jobs" based on Steve Jobs' life. I must say, he is an example of a person that was truly committed to his cause of creating technology that is of an advanced level. Sometimes your vision and commitment to excellence will not make sense to anyone but you, and that is okay. I recall in the movie, Ashton Kutcher, who was Steve Jobs' character say, "You do not accept things as they are. Never stop innovating. You got to have a problem that you want to solve, or a wrong that you want to right. It's got to be something you're passionate about or otherwise you won't have the perseverance to see it through. Do not look at the competition, and say you will do it better. Say you will do it differently". Steve Jobs was so dedicated to the company Apple that at times his commitment to the product was too much to handle for some people. At one point, he was even fired from Apple, the company that he built and started. However, this did not deter Steve Jobs. He kept his focus and commitment to creating an excellent product.

In the Bible, Ruth, is perfect example of commitment to excellence. At the time, Ruth probably did not realize what impact her commitment to Naomi would mean to her life. *And Ruth said, "Urge me not to leave you or to turn back from following you; for where you go I will go, and where you lodge I will lodge. Your people shall be my people and your God my God. Where you die I will die, and there will I be buried. The Lord do so to me, and more also, if anything but death parts me from you."* When Naomi saw that Ruth was determined to go with her, she said no more (Ruth 1:16-18 AMP). Due to her commitment of being faithful to Naomi, she met her future husband Boaz. Ruth's life was forever changed!

When we are committed to excellence, we go the distance and take no shortcuts.

134

Committed to excellence is also honoring that which we say we are committed. I also find that when we are committed to excellence, we don't have time to grumble and complain. Why? Because you are so focused and zoned into accomplishing a task in an excellent manner. I can vividly recall a time I was it attendance at a meeting and the atmosphere was so negative. People were murmuring and complaining. As I looked around, I couldn't help but think to myself, "Why are they complaining? Where is their commitment to excellence?" If you were fully committed to this, your focus would be on doing an excellent job instead of complaining about miniscule things. Often, people will complain, and do nothing to change their situation. When you are committed to excellence, complaining does not have a place.

Excellent Requires Timeliness

When we are in the will of God for our lives, and fulfilling our purpose, we are diligent and focused on what is before us. Excellence requires that we do a task in a timely manner. When you are in the pursuit of excellence, there is no room for procrastination. Procrastination is the enemy of success. Procrastination will throw you off course. Often, the things people procrastinate with are things that require immediate attention. Procrastination halts progress. Instead of getting to a task and completing it with excellence, you delay it to a later time. Sometimes that time never comes. Also, when you procrastinate, you make more work for yourself in the long run. Then when you finally get to the task, you are all stressed out because of procrastination. When you procrastinate, it demonstrates that you are irresponsible.

When I think of procrastination, I think of Jonah. Jonah knew that there was a call on his life. He did whatever he could do to avoid that call. He procrastinated in his call and attempted to run from God because He believed God required too much from him. Now, if you have not realized, you cannot outrun God. God had to get Jonah's attention. God allowed for Jonah to be swallowed by a whale. After learning his lesson, Jonah finally stopped procrastinating.

When we operate in a timely fashion, God will reward our faithfulness. I also believe in the natural sense because is beneficial to our lives to be timely. I have a friend who works in corporate America. She told me how recently she received a promotion at work. She believes one of the factors in her receiving a promotion is that she is timely in everything that she does on the job. She elaborated more and said that whatever tasks she is assigned she completes them before they are due. She also encourages her other coworkers to do the same. Excellence requires timeliness and this will in turn cause elevation on many levels.

Excellent Requires Sacrifice

To sacrifice means to give up something, for the sake of something better. In order for your dreams and goals to come to fruition, it will require some sort of sacrifice on your part. I remember when I was a Music Education major at Hofstra University, and I realized that I wanted to excel at my studies and continue to play the flute well. Besides, my parents were paying hefty tuition fees for me to attend Hofstra University. I recall one time one of my fellow flutists asked if I wanted to hang out with a few other people that weekend. I forgo going to the party so that I could stay in my dorm room and practice and complete some homework assignments. When you are committed to doing everything with excellence, you will have to sacrifice some things. I remember sacrificing parties or other social events for the sake of being excellent at what I did. Today, I am the same way. I have goals that I know in order for them to fully come to pass, it will require sacrifice on my part. As I work on completing my music projects and this book, I have had to make some sacrifices. Guess what? I am fine with that. Sometimes, I turn down invitations to places because it will take time away from me moving toward my goal. I realize a temporary sacrifice will yield a greater reward in the long term.

Abraham, who was named Abram, before he received the call from God is a good biblical example of sacrificing in pursuit of excellence. He sacrificed leaving all he knew to go to a new land that God showed him. *The Lord said to Abram, "Go from your country, your people and your father's household to the land I will show you"* (Genesis 12:1 NIV). Many times when you are sacrificing for your dream and goals, people may not understand. You have to be determined to stay focused and keep sacrificing and know that God will reward you for doing your part.

Recently, I joined a network marketing program. Also, I have participated in various ones in the past. I believe in multiple streams of income. My mentor has been in this program for over a year. He is very successful! What I have observed with him are his tremendous sacrifices. One time, I asked the latest time I could call if I had any questions or needed any information. He blew my mind when said he didn't have a cut off time for phone calls! My mentor has done membership calls into the early hours of the morning in the past! He said when you have a vision, you have to make sacrifices. If you do not, it will not come to pass. He spends hours on personal development, sleeps little, and dedicates a lot of time to our team. He realizes in order for himself and the team to be successful, he had to make some sacrifices.

There is this saying, "Grind Now, Shine Later". Grind in the urban term, means: "to work hard, keep pressing forward, make moves that will benefit you, and always purposefully doing things to make money." In order to be true to the *grind*, you have to sacrifice. To be excellent, you must make sacrifices now that will benefit you later.

I created an acronym for the word grind- **G**o **R**egardless **I**n spite of **N**onsense **D**aily. As long as you are living on this earth, you are going to encounter nonsense or distractions. You may encounter things that will upset you or irritate you and try to discourage you from pursuing excellence in all that you do, but regardless you have to press forward in spite of the nonsense. You have to be so driven and determined to see your goals come to pass. Resolve in your spirit, that you will press forward and keep going towards the mark. When you decide to sacrifice and "grind", you will make moves with such determination that you make things happen!   There will be challenges, but as you press through them, you will be better for it. You will learn lessons that will enhance your life, so GRIND!

Use Your Gifts

In doing everything with excellence, you must use your God-given gifts. God gives us gifts so that we may put them to use. So many people have gifts that are lying dormant within. We are blessed to be blessings. Our gifts can be a blessing to someone else. Remember the parable of the talents. God gave each one of them different talents. Each person was to put his gifts to use. All of them, except for one, obeyed God and used their gift. The one person that did not use their gift, God called them a wicked and lazy servant. You see when you use your gifts, God blesses you with more gifts. Utilizing your gifts in an excellent manner brings abundance to your life. When you use your gifts, you honor God with your life, and He will open doors for you that no man can shut!

In everything that you do, no matter how great or small, you need to do it with excellence.

Celebrate Other People

Zig Ziglar, a famous author, once said, "You can have everything in life you want if you will just help enough other people get what they want." I truly believe when we celebrate the accomplishments of other people, it opens the doors of success for ourselves. When we are happy for the success of others, it allows us to be a receiver of blessings. Whatever we sow, we shall reap. This is why it is good to be happy for others. What God has allowed for someone else, He can also make it happen for you. Remember, He is no respecter of persons.

Keys to Remember

- Strive for excellence in all that you do
- Spending time with God is key in knowing how to do things excellently
- Excellence requires commitment
- Excellence requires timeliness
- Excellence requires sacrifice
- Use your gifts in pursuit of excellence
- God rewards excellence

Chapter 9

FORGIVE OTHERS

"Be gentle and forbearing with one another, and if one has a difference (a grievance or complaint) against another, readily pardoning each other; even as the Lord had [freely] forgiven you, so must you also [forgive]."
(Colossians 3:13 AMP)

While writing this book, this is the most difficult chapter I had to write. When you are hurt almost beyond repair, it's not easy to express that on paper. I had experienced one of the worst betrayals that a woman may experience.

I was in love with the love of my life. We had dated for several years. I loved him with my whole heart and soul. I couldn't go a day without seeing him. I needed to be with him. I would try to spend all my time with him. This happened quite often at the expense of putting my own needs aside. We dated for several years. We were in love. I truly believe God showed me signs to not proceed forward and that he was not the one, but of course, I did not listen. There were signs of infidelity and immaturity, but I chose to ignore it. Iyanla Vanzant once said, "When you don't deal with what's going on, it keeps going on."

After several years of dating him, he proposed to me. We got engaged! I was so happy! Although, something inside of me did not feel quite right, there was a bit of uneasiness. I chucked it up as being pre-wedding jitters. As months led up to the wedding, something inside of me was saying, "call it off", and "do not go through with this." At this point, I didn't know how to call it off. The invitations had already went out, and we already were in contract for our house! Even though I loved my fiancé at the time, I did not trust him when it came to other women. The previous years had been racked with me finding out about various inappropriate "friendships" he had with other women. Also, he loved to party and frequently went out to clubs. Even still, our wedding arrived. I remember our wedding day. It was such a beautiful day filled with family and friends.

It is a problem when you start your marriage like roommates. There was his money, and my money. If he bought a chair for the house, I would owe him half the amount of the chair. One of the biggest issues in our marriage, was over $5000. For the record, it was my money. Several years later, I became pregnant. As I said in an earlier chapter, I had a miscarriage, which was so devastating. But, about two months later, I became pregnant with our son, who I later named Matthew. 2010 was my best and worst year simultaneously! The best, because my son was born, and the worst because my marriage was falling apart. My marriage was going down like The Titanic! Months leading up to delivering Matthew, it was quite difficult between us because we were constantly arguing. I remember those times, being quite trying. I felt very alone in our marriage. At my baby shower, I remember him and I putting up a good front as if all was well. However, that was far from the truth. I remember the night of my baby shower, coming home alone because we drove separate cars. When I got home, he was not home, and I remember crying myself to sleep that night. I was so hurt and angry about various things in our marriage. Also, I was dealing with the fact that I had just learned that he had another child, which was conceived while we were engaged to be married. I had so many emotions raging inside-anger, hurt, disappointment, and betrayal. Because of this, I started to have self-doubt and started to question myself as to what I did wrong that lead to him treating me this way. I felt like a fool and a failure. I was ashamed and hopeless.

Months later, I finally gave birth to my precious little boy. Things were still not quite right with his father and me. I felt like we were just coexisting and not living in a marriage together. I was in a loveless marriage. After having Matthew, the fighting with his father and I escalated as there was tension in the house. I felt like he did want me no longer as a wife and was stressed that he had not 1 but 2 children to handle. The stress of being a new mom and my marital issues were too much for me. Even though I would smile through my pain, I felt myself slipping into depression. I truly thank God for my parents. There were with me every step of the way and made sure that Matthew and I were taken care of.

One day, I remember I was at home and sobbing as I sat on the couch. At that point, my friend Cherise called me. I told her how I was feeling and she invited me to bible study. She mentioned to me that Oslyn, a friend of ours, would be there, too. Cherise also told me that I would meet her friend Dina and her parents. I loved the Lord and knew that God never fails. I realized I needed help. I accepted her invitation. I never knew that attending this bible study would change my life forever!

I arrived to Dina's house and parked. I rang the doorbell and Dina's mom, Mrs. Skeffrey, answered the door. I introduced myself as she warmly welcomed me in her home. I proceeded to follow her into the family room. There were several people seated there. Mrs. Skeffrey introduced me to Minister Vivian Allen, who was leading the bible study. I remember listening to her teach; she was so knowledgeable about the word. I honestly cannot say what she taught on that day because my head was in a fog. Before ending the bible study, Vivian, as we called her, looked at me and said, "Dara, you've been pulling on my spirit throughout the whole bible study." She began to tell me things about my life and marriage and the tears began streaming down my face. She was prophetic and a minister of a deliverance ministry. I remember looking at Dina who was sitting at the dining room table. The whole time she just looked at me with sadness in her eyes. As Vivian began to speak to me, I continued to cry. She laid hands on me and prayed for me. The next thing I know, I fell off the couch and onto the floor. At this point, I remember, Mrs. Skeffrey, Cherise, and Oslyn, surrounding me and praying for me. I felt as if something lifted off of me. It was almost like a rebirth. After this prayer, I felt stronger. As the months continued, I knew I needed to attend this bible study. I knew that God's word has life giving power, and I needed to be surrounded by God's word as much as possible. *"My son, attend to my words; consent and submit to my sayings. Let them not depart from your sight; keep them in the center of your heart. For they are life to those who find them, healing and health to all their flesh"* (Proverbs 4:20-22 AMP). I truly believe God ordered my steps to be there at the bible study and meet everyone. This was a divine connection. As time went on, I began to meet some powerful women of God. These women spoke life back into my spirit when I was down. They were gifts from God. They began to speak prophetically to me about the wonderful things that God would do and had planned for my life. I was astounded because these women never met me before, but they knew things about me. I knew it was God. Only God can reveal such things.

Trials and Tribulations

The next several months, I had some good days and bad days. There were times when I was fine, and other times when I was not. At times, I was still depressed, but not as much as before. I began to have hope again. I remember while going through this valley, I attended bible study faithfully and would attend as many services as possible. I often took

Matthew with me. I knew that in order to get passed this hurdle in my life, I had to walk with God every step of the way. I needed to indulge myself on His word and His promises for my life. At home, my marriage was still in shambles and falling apart. We were so opposite, like two ships passing in the night. We no longer talked to each other. We would say a few words to each other here and there, but that was all. It seemed as if all communication had ceased. The tension was so great, that I decided to not stay in our bedroom. We continued to argue, and he became verbally abusive. His anger at times, scared me. I decided to start sleeping in our guest bedroom. I put Matthew's bassinet in the room with me so that he could be with me at all times. Right then, I began to feel like a single mother. I felt like I could not count on him as a husband. I was taking care of Matthew for the most part by myself. At times, it was overwhelming. I thank God that my parents were there to help and support me in any way they could. I was truly glad that during this time, I stayed out of work on maternity leave. I do not think I could have handled being a new mom, teaching, and the stress of my out of control marriage. It would have been too great a feat to deal with it. Throughout this time, I continued to attend bible study and worship services. I thank God for sending me Tomekia, my prayer partner, who I met at our bible study. Tomekia and I would pray on the phone early in the morning around 6AM whatever concerns we had, and we would take them to the Lord in prayer. Prayer works and God hears our prayers. Praying and attending the bible study was strengthening me little by little. I cannot say that at this time, I was completely over my depression. My marriage was still a hot mess!!! It's amazing because I put on a good front, for people who did not know the chaos that surrounded my life at the time. Even though I was smiling and seemed happy to the outside world, inside I felt like dying. I kept asking myself, "Why me? What did I do to deserve a bad marriage? Why doesn't my husband love and desire me?" And on and on the questions went. The self-doubt and confusion began to crowd my mind. Even though I had the most precious and amazing baby, I felt hopeless. I felt like my life was not going to get better. I could not see better days ahead. The depression began to get worse. Please understand the demons of depression are real. The sad part was that at the time, as much as I smiled, I also cried. I felt alone and sad. I knew the Lord and loved God so much. I just wanted the pain to go away.

From Bad to Worse

I had stayed home with my son for about 8 months on maternity leave. The ninth month arrived and it was September. This month marked my arrival back to work. As I look back, I don't know if it was the pressure of going back to work and leaving my baby that made me feel overwhelmed. At work, I tried as best as I could to focus on my students and allow them to become the best musicians they could be. At home, my marriage was still rocky because we hardly spoke to one another. We only talked when it was necessary. It was really a sad situation. At work, I tried to always smile and be friendly. Yet inside, I felt so incomplete and lost. I totally felt like a loser. I wanted the pain to stop. I slowly but surely began to check out. However, I was able to mask it well. I remember feeling completely overwhelmed and sad. My depression started to become despair. I felt like such a failure. I now know that it was a lie from the pit of hell, but as I was going through it, I did not believe so. The sadness that I felt in my heart began to overtake me. My prayers of God helped me as I began to turn to God and cry out for Him to please take this pain away. My prayer actually went like this: "God, I know heaven is a wonderful place, and I want to be with you. I cannot take this life anymore, I feel hopeless." Over the next few days, that became my prayer. I was still crying myself to sleep at night. That became a common occurrence for me. I did not talk to my parents about this because I knew they were heartbroken over my situation as it affected my family. The whole situation completely tore my family apart.

The day came that I decided I couldn't take it anymore. I remember pulling up into my driveway, and I sat there. I began to cry and weep, meanwhile, Matthew was asleep in his car seat. Something within me said turn off the car and go inside. I remember going inside my house. I put Matthew down and put my purse on the couch. I sat on the couch, and I continued to cry. This time my cries got louder, and I sobbed and sobbed. At that point, my cell phone rang, I looked at it and saw that it was my pastor calling me. I thought to myself, I cannot answer this call, I am a mess, and I am crying. I felt the Holy Spirit, tell me to answer it. I picked up the phone and said hello. I will never forget her words that day. She said, "Dara, are you ok?" I did not answer her, and I began to sob even harder. She continued, "I was laying on the couch taking a nap, and the Holy Spirit woke me and said, "Get up, someone you know is deeply troubled." My pastor jumped up and asked, "Who?" The Holy Spirit showed her my face. After that, all I know is that my pastor went into warfare mode. She prayed the depression away from me. I literally felt my body feeling lighter. It felt like I was on the phone with her for hours when it probably was an hour. By the end of our phone call, I was laughing, feeling jovial, and looking forward to the future. I praise God! Since that day, I have never felt such despair as I did before. I know that it was God that relieved my pain.

God healed my heart

As months went forward, God began to heal my heart from the hurt and the pain. *He heals the brokenhearted and binds up their wounds* (Psalm 147:3 NKJV). It was a slow and gradual process but I realized that in order to move forward with my life, I had to let go of the pain from the past. *"I do not consider, brethren, that I have captured and made it my own (yet); but one thing I do (it is my one aspiration): forgetting what lies behind and straining forward to what lies ahead"* (Philippians 3:13 AMP).

Forgiveness, why is it so hard? Is it because when we think about forgiving others, we feel like we are relinquishing our power? Forgiveness is really about freeing you and not the person who wronged you. Once you are free from the hurt and anger you can move forward with your life. Holding on to unforgiveness does not hurt the other person, it hurts you! Meanwhile, the person who hurt you has moved on and is living their life. The Bible also calls us to be at peace with one another (Hebrews 12:14). When you allow the hurt to fester, it does not leave room for healing. I truly believe once you forgive, you open the doors to God's goodness in your life. It was not until I was able to forgive, that I was able to see things from a different perspective. Remember, forgiveness is not about the other person, it is about you. If I were to stay hurt, bitter, and angry it would not hurt him, it would hurt me. In order for me to move on with my life, and press in to all that God has for me, I had to forgive. I know what anger and hurt feels like to the point you cannot see straight. You actually feel like you're seeing red! Do not allow anger to be a hindrance to your blessings, prosperity, and advancement. Sometimes, those old feelings of hurt come back from time to time, and I have to remind myself to keep them in check, and move forward. I have bigger fish to fry! I have a call of God on my life. I have things to do, places to go, people to meet, and my destiny to accomplish!!! In the words of Sweet Brown, "Ain't nobody got time for that!" I truly do not want my anger or ill feelings to hinder any blessings that God may have for me. My dear friends, I encourage you to do the same thing. Let go of past hurts, let go of people who wronged you. Sometimes, you have to be alright with a sorry you may never get. God is not sleeping. He sees it all. Let God deal with them and go on and live your life to the fullest! As Paul said in the book of Philippians, to forget those things which lie behind and press forward toward the mark!

Keys to Remember

- Forgiveness sets you free
- When you forgive you feel less stress and anxiety
- Forgiveness helps to release disturbing thoughts
- Allow the peace of God to rule in your mind, heart, and thoughts
- Allow the Holy Spirit to minister to you
- As a believer, we are to forgive others, just as God forgives us

Chapter 10

EXERCISE WISDOM

"Wisdom is the principal thing; therefore get wisdom: and with all thy getting get understanding".
(Proverbs 4:7)

Wisdom is seeking God for every matter of your life. *"O God, thou art my God; early will I seek thee: my soul thirsteth for thee, my flesh longeth for thee in a dry and thirsty land, where no water is."* (Psalm 63:1). Often, we talk to everyone else about our situations or problems except God. Remember, God sees the ins and outs of our lives. He sees the things we cannot see. When you walk with God and exercise His wisdom, God will reveal your true life's purpose. You

162

will begin to understand why certain things happened and why certain things did not happen.

When you drive to a destination for the first time, you may use your GPS. You rely on your GPS and trust that it will get you to where you need to go. You do not question the GPS nor wonder how or if it will work because you are assured that it will do what it needs to do. So, why then, with something as great and tremendous as your life, would you not rely on God, who created you and knows exactly how to get you to your divine destination? *If any of you lacks wisdom, let him ask of God, who gives to all liberally and without reproach, and it will be given to him* (James 1:5 NKJV). Solomon, one of the greatest rulers in The Bible, could have asked God for anything, but the one thing he asked for was wisdom.

Listen to God's Voice

In order to listen to God's voice, you need to seek Him in prayer. Pray about everything! God will give you the wisdom, strategy, and the answers you seek for anything in your life. He will also give you discernment about the situations in your life. Like a film writer, God knows the script of your life.

I recall in my own life, when I did not listen to God's wisdom and the results were deep hurt and disappointment. *My people are destroyed for lack of knowledge* (Hosea 4:6 NKJV). I am going to be transparent with what I am about to say. If my story can prevent another woman from going through what I went through, so be it. God told me not get married. He gave me signs upon signs, but I did not listen. While we dated, there were various women that I found out about, but still I proceeded to get married to him. The blessing that came from this union was my son. I thank God for my son every day. But, I do regret not heeding God's voice. I had the mindset that if I loved him more, gave more of myself, become sweeter than I already was, that he would change, and forsake all others. I remember when we dated, I would plan my day around him and even cancel plans with friends, just in case he wanted to spend time with me. I know it sounds absolutely ridiculous, but that was the frame of mind I was operating in. It was like my life revolved around him!

Love Yourself

One thing I learned from this, is that after God, you have to love yourself. If you do not love yourself, who will? If you do not set boundaries and expectations on how you want to be treated, be prepared to be mistreated. I know I am not the only woman who has endured this. Often times, we as women forget ourselves and take care of everyone else's needs before our own. Yes, it is good to have a kind and giving heart, but not at the expense of your well- being. I believe God calls us to be docile, but not doormats. *If you let people treat you like a doormat, you'll be quite forgotten in the end* (Proverbs 29:21 MSG). Do not allow any person to abuse or misuse you. You are a child of the Most High God and should be loved and cherished accordingly. We teach people how to treat us by what we allow.

It is important to love yourself. Know that you have worth and value. Do not settle for the sake of being in a relationship. For the preservation of myself, I had to change. I could no longer operate under my previous ways. This was doing more harm than good for me. I have learned that setting expectations and boundaries make for healthy and happy relationships.

Before you make any decisions or make any moves, seek God's wisdom. Remember, wisdom is the principal thing. When writing this chapter, God revealed to me 5 areas in which I need to exercise wisdom. I like to call them my 5 M's.

Ministry

You may be wondering why is ministry one of my 5 M's when I am not a minister. Well, anyone who believes and receives Jesus as Lord and Savior is called to minister. Plus, our relationship with God needs to come first before any other relationship. Make God a priority in your life. Often, when we think about ministry, we think of someone who is serving people from a pulpit. But, ministry encompasses so much more than that. There are so many different ways that we are called to serve the body of Christ and to minister to unbelievers as well. One of Jesus' first mandates was the Great Commission. "*Go therefore and make disciples of all the nations, baptizing them in the name of the Father and of the Son and of the Holy Spirit*" (Matthew 28:19 NKJV).

One of my gifts in ministry is to encourage others. As best I can, I try to encourage others to fulfill their God – given purpose. Also, writing this book is a part of my ministry. God gave me the vision and revelation to write this book.

Matthew

My precious little boy, I thank God for him every day. He is the reason why I grind and press forward. I work hard so that he will not have to. I pray that his future will be even better and brighter than mine. I pray that He will walk in all the gifts that God has bestowed upon him. I pray that He will fulfill the call of God on his life. For those of you who have children, I believe you feel the same way. My son is the reason I keep moving forward even when I do not want to do so. Matthew is a gift from God to me. I ask God daily to give me wisdom in raising my son. I pray that I am being the best mother to him as possible.

Matters of the Heart

I thank God for my family, and my friends. They are matters of the heart to me. I am thankful that I come from a strong and supportive family. They are blessing to me in so many ways. I pray for my family daily and thank God for them.

I thank God for wonderful and supportive friends as well. It has been said that you cannot choose your family, but you can choose your friends. This is an area in which you must exercise wisdom. Surrounding yourself with the wrong people can be a detriment to your destiny. *As iron sharpens iron, so one person sharpens another* (Proverbs 27:17). Birds of a feather truly do flock together. Often people with no purpose, gravitate to other people who do not have a vision. Successful people on the other hand, link up with other successful people. It is important that you evaluate your friendships. If your goal is to be successful, do not walk with mediocrity. They will not understand your purpose or vision. When you walk with wise men or women, you will be wise. Remember, iron sharpens iron. If the friendships you have are not encouraging you to fulfill your God- given purpose, then you need to do some reevaluating in regards to those friendships. If the people you are around have no vision, purpose, focus, or discipline, then you need to change your circle. The Bible says, "How can two walk together unless they agree?" I truly believe it is important to surround yourself with like-minded people. People who have a vision for their life, will encourage you to do the same. They will not try to block or hinder your progress. Remember, this is your life. Only you can make the significant changes that you seek.

I also believe in exercising wisdom when seeking a spouse. From my own experience, not heeding God's voice caused me deep heartache and pain. The Bible speaks of being equally yoked (2 Corinthians 6:14) with a person. Often, when we hear this term, we think of being yoked spiritually. I believe you should look at all areas when choosing a mate. For example, what are their views about money? Are they selfish with money or generous? Do they spend frivolously or wisely? Look at their family dynamics. Is their family harmonious or dysfunctional? How do they treat their friends? What are their work ethics? These are just a few key areas to evaluate and reflect upon when choosing a mate. I believe we do not have to figure these things out on our own. If you seek

God's wisdom, He will give you all the answers you need. When it comes to your life, you must exercise wisdom. This is not the time to become complacent and let the chips fall where they may. I urge and compel you to exercise wisdom in all areas of your life, but especially with the people you choose to associate with.

Music

Music has always been a major part of my life. I love music and cannot see my life without it. I enjoy teaching music, but playing my flute is my passion. I am truly thankful for the many opportunities in music that God has afforded me. As I said in an earlier chapter, God gave me the vision for Dara Marie Productions, which is the name of my band. The Bible says, that if you lack wisdom, ask God. God gives us wisdom

173

for every area of my life. I always seek God for ideas musically, and for which music ventures to pursue. He always answers. I am truly thankful for the team of people that God has placed in my life, to help push my music forward.

Money

This is an area in which you must exercise wisdom. When it comes to money, if you do not exercise wisdom, it will not bode well with you. I have heard people say that money is evil. Money by itself is not evil. It is what you do with it, that it can become evil. *For the love of money is a root of all kinds of evil, for which some have strayed from the faith in their greediness, and pierced themselves through with many sorrows* (1 Timothy 6:10 NKJV). Money is a tool. It takes money to fund the gospel. It takes money to eliminate poverty, homelessness, and many other ills of society. When you exercise wisdom as it comes to money, you will not only benefit yourself, but you may benefit others as well.

A very successful business man shared a great piece of knowledge with me. "When it comes to your business and business ventures, watch what everyone else is doing and do the complete opposite. Be a leader not a follower. Usually following the crowd will lead to a dead- end destination." I read an anonymous quote that said, "Let them sleep while you grind. Let them party while you work. Let them see the difference in the results." I have also learned that if your money is not working for you, it is working against you. Find ways to invest and grow your money. I also believe that your financial freedom will happen when you focus on the gifts that God gave you. By exercising wisdom, you will attain your God-given dreams.

Keys to Remember

- Wisdom is the principal thing

- Wisdom is the power of right judgment

- Obtaining wisdom should be the greatest goal in life

- Exercising wisdom is knowing how to think, speak, and act before God and man

- Without wisdom, people make poor choices

- Wisdom allows us to make wise decisions

- Wisdom is the basis for victorious living

Conclusion

When we are born we come into this world alone, and ultimately we die alone. I want you to know that God's love for you is everlasting. His Word is true; He will never leave you nor forsake you. He does not have ulterior motives. He has your best interest at heart. You never have to second- guess with God. He will not play games with your heart. He is straightforward. He says what He means and He means what He says. Just read His word and you will find this to be true for yourself. God's word and love never fails. He will make your crooked places straight. He will guard you and keep you in all your ways. He has a good plan for your life. God loves you so much that He knows the numbers of hairs on your head. Think about that for a moment. Can you fathom His love? Please understand, I am talking about having a relationship with God. Religion at times confuses people and gives them a distorted view of who God is. A relationship with God brings clarity, hope, and a resolve to press forward. When you *walk with God* you will never be disappointed. I am not saying that life becomes trouble free, but you can have the confidence in knowing that you will not be overcome by the situations in your life.

If you have never accepted Jesus as your Lord and Savior, and would like to, please pray this prayer:

Salvation Prayer

Father God, I believe that Jesus died for me, so that I may have eternal life. I accept Him as my Lord and Savior. Please forgive me of my sins. Come into my heart and show me the right way to live. In Jesus' name, Amen!

If you prayed this prayer, believe God heard you and now look forward to a wonderful walk with God! Be blessed!